PROJECTS
IN
LESS TIME
A SYNOPSIS OF CRITICAL CHAIN

MARK J. WOEPPEL

Pinnacle Strategies Publication 2006

Mark Woeppel
President & CEO | Pinnacle Strategies
3600 Lowrey Way . Plano . Texas . 75025

ISBN: 1-4196-2053-3

All Rights © 2006 by Mark J. Woeppel

Illustrations by Daniel J. Frey

Published by Pinnacle Strategies

Printed in the USA

www.pinnacle-strategies.com

TABLE OF CONTENTS

APPENDIX

INTRODUCTION

The purpose of this book is to provide an overview of the Critical Chain project management solution. I've used Eliyahu Goldratt's book, **Critical Chain,** as a framework to help you understand the main components of the solution. Therefore, this book attempts to be a faithful synopsis of his book. While the synopses of the **Critical Chain** chapters in this book are limited to the concepts expressed in Goldratt's original text, I added my own observations and interpretations to enhance your understanding. **Projects in Less Time** provides an introduction to the ideas introduced by **Critical Chain** in an easy-to-digest form and then rounds it out with glossary terms, and reference materials.

According to many project management professionals, Goldratt's **Critical Chain** is "required reading." It's thought to be the most significant contribution to project management since the introduction of the PERT system and the critical path method.

There are many, many, examples of organizations that have benefited from these methods (there is a sampling in the appendix), from product development, to construction, to software. I hope that when you read this, you'll gain an appreciation for the logical, tested foundation for the critical chain solution and by understanding; you'll be able to improve your project performance.

ABOUT THE AUTHOR

Many people, including Eliyahu Goldratt himself, consider Mark J. Woeppel to be a leading expert on the Theory of Constraints (ToC). He has been involved in the development and implementation of ToC since the mid-1980's, as one of the first in the world to implement drum-buffer-rope. Woeppel is President and CEO of Pinnacle Strategies, a multinational consulting and software firm headquartered in the United States in Plano, Texas. With successful projects on three continents to his credit, Woeppel is known for his exceptional ability to improve businesses. He is a popular keynote speaker and welcome lecturer on a variety of management techniques including Theory of Constraints (ToC), Critical Chain project management, supply chain management and drum-buffer-rope. Woeppel's workshops and seminars deliver a full complement of course offerings from sales to critical chain and are attended by leaders of companies around the world. In 2002 Woeppel developed ManuSync™, an Advanced Planning and Scheduling (APS) and management decision support software tool for manufacturers.

Projects in Less Time is Woeppel's second book. He is also the author of **Manufacturer's Guide to Implementing the Theory of Constraints** which, since its publication by St. Lucie Press in 2001 (ISBN:1574442686), has remained the definitive step-by-step handbook on how to implement ToC in manufacturing. The guide shows readers how to answer the question, "What in my business has to change in order for it to be successful?" Packed with relevant advice and real world examples, it offers readers a complete implementation checklist, sample policies, and procedures documents. It has been translated into Japanese, Korean, and Spanish.

ABOUT ELIYAHU M. GOLDRATT AND CRITICAL CHAIN

ELIYAHU GOLDRATT

Physicist turned business writer and corporate consultant, Eliyahu M. Goldratt is the author of **Critical Chain**, the book upon which **Projects in Less Time** is based. He is credited with creating the Theory of Constraints (ToC), a business methodology that transforms management thinking and results in dramatically improved business performance.

Born in 1948 in Israel and educated there, Goldratt obtained his Bachelor of Science degree from Tel Aviv University and his Masters of Science and Doctorate of Philosophy from Bar-Llan University. He holds patents for inventions ranging from medical devices to sensors, is the author of eight books and is a regular contributor to scientific and business publications. He has created an eight-session CD-ROM educational series on ToC as well as a self-learning kit to help organizations learn ToC. Eliyahu Goldratt founded the Avraham Y. Goldratt Institute which is internationally known for the development of new business management philosophies and systems, from which he is now retired in order to spend more time writing, lecturing and consulting. Companies that have retained Goldratt for his business expertise include General Motors, Proctor & Gamble, AT&T, NV Philips and Boeing.

As often as Goldratt is identified as a leader with fresh vision of incalculable value, he is labeled as unconventional and idiosyncratic. Regardless of how you describe this popular educator, scientist and philosopher, it's undeniable that his ideas will change how you think about business.

THE BOOK, CRITICAL CHAIN

Published in 1997 by North River Press (ISBN: 0884271536), **Critical Chain**, like Goldratt's widely acclaimed first book on business, **The Goal**, is a business book disguised as a novel. Goldratt endeavors to accomplish a number of different objectives in **Critical Chain**. His primary purpose is, of course, to educate readers about the critical chain concept, but he also uses this book to question the relevance of some strongly ingrained basic assumptions, not just in the area of business, but in business education as well.

A young associate university professor who teaches project management on the post graduate level is a central character in **Critical Chain**, as is his colleague who teaches in the same Executive MBA program. The colleague has just returned from a sabbatical; a year long consulting assignment for a company that actively uses ToC and is known for impressive expansion and profits. As the story unfolds, the young professor is researching new techniques for a paper he is writing and the returning colleague shares powerful new concepts he learned while on sabbatical. The project management professor and his students gain depth and breadth of understanding together as the students begin to use Theory of Constraints methods in their business "day jobs." Also instrumental to the plot are three students who are concurrently employed by a modem maker. They are singled out by their company to form a task force and charged with the responsibility of reducing the manufacturer's product development time. As they succeed, we, the readers gain more and more insight into the major tenets of ToC and Critical Chain. Meanwhile, Goldratt weaves his opinions about education into the text through the concerns of the university president who struggles with declining business school enrollments.

MAJOR CRITICAL CHAIN CHARACTERS

In their Order of Appearance

Daniel Pullman and **Isaac Levy** are the co-founders of Genemodem, a modem manufacturer concerned with staying ahead of the competition.

Genemodem Think Tank is a task force comprised of an unconventional young engineer, brand manager, and project auditor from Genemodem. They are challenged by their company to increase market share by shortening product development time. The three are also students in Professor Rick Silver's project management course at the university.

Rick Silver is an associate professor who teaches the Project Management course in the Executive MBA program at the university.

Mark is one of Professor Silver's students and the leader of the Genemodem Think Tank trio.

BJ von Braun is president of the university where Professor Rick Silver teaches and she is very concerned about sagging business school enrollments.

Jim is Professor Silver's department head at the university.

Johnny Fisher is a full professor who teaches a course in the MBA program at the university. He has just returned from a one year sabbatical during which he consulted at UniCo, a company known for exceptional expansion and profits.

Don Pederson is an especially high powered UniCo VP.

Fred is a member of the Genemodem Think Tank.

Ruth is a member of the Genemodem Think Tank.

Charlene is an accounting professor at the university.

Ted is one of Professor Silver's project management course students.

Brad Newbolt is the president of Q.E.C., a company where one of Professor Silver's students works.

CHAPTER
SUMMARIES & COMMENTARIES
CHAPTER 1 – THERE IS A PROBLEM AT GENEMODEM

We are introduced to Genemodem, the company Goldratt uses as an example throughout the book. The company's founders, Daniel Pullman, the board chairman and CEO and Isaac Levy, the executive VP of engineering, discuss the fact that Genemodem has been successful, but in order to continue to dominate the competition, the company must make exceptional reductions in the time it takes to develop and introduce new products. An outside consultant has made many recommendations, but Pullman suspects that even all those enhancements combined would only produce, at most, a 5% decrease in the time it takes Genemodem to get a new product to market.

Rather than act on the consultant's suggestions, Pullman and Levy realize they need a more powerful solution. They launch a "think tank" made up of a carefully selected trio of their own young, unconventional in-company managers: an engineer, a brand manager and a project auditor from accounting. They issue a specific challenge to the newly formed group: to increase Genemodem's share in a market moving at breakneck speed — and to do it by shortening development time.

Genemodem's products have a life span of only about six months — a life span that will continue to shrink if not offset by a similarly short duration for product development. In fact, we read that, disturbingly, the company's development time is running at about two years. So, it is painfully obvious that at some time in the future Genemodem will either introduce an inferior product that beats a competitor's introduction or a good product that trails a competitor's launch by months. Missing the market will mean that the Genemodem share price will take a nosedive. A second market miss will cause so much damage that the company may not survive.

THE THINK TANK

The think tank trio will test their new approaches on the new A226 modem which is currently in the product development stage. They will have an unrestricted budget, decision-making authority, and a deadline of 16 months. If they succeed, 10,000 shares of company stock will be awarded to each of them.

Following up on one of the few concrete hints their VP gave them about how to proceed, the trio promptly enrolls in an executive MBA program at a local university.

COMMENTARY – CHAPTER I

What is the implication of managing projects badly? It isn't that they're just late or over budget. Projects are supposed to produce significant business results — new products, new processes, and sometimes, even the product itself is the result of a project. How well we manage projects has a profound impact on the success of our organization.

In the story, we are introduced to a high tech company, an environment where rapid product innovation is critical to the long-term success of the company. Thus, we arrive at the problem statement for the book: how can project performance be *radically* improved — shortened? In the story, we are faced with one of the most demanding environments (in terms of speed), the rapidly changing technology market.

This product development project is only one example of how significantly reducing lead time and gaining the ability to reliably hit a specific project completion date can impact the viability of a firm. This is the promise of **Critical Chain** — to improve the ability to reduce project lead times and finish on time.

GLOSSARY – CHAPTER I

Project

- ∞ A plan or proposal; a scheme.
- ∞ An undertaking requiring concerted effort such as a community cleanup project or a government-funded irrigation project.

Project performance — The ability of a project to match pre-established criteria.

CHAPTER 2 – MEET RICK SILVER

Rick Silver, an ambitious young associate professor who has been waiting for an opportunity to shine, is selected to teach the project management course in his university's Executive MBA Program. He was chosen for his unusual open discussion style of teaching because his school hoped it would be especially appealing to students dealing with real-world problems.

COMMENTARY – CHAPTER 2

The university sub plot deals with the nature of business education and has nothing to do with projects. Here, we're introduced to our protagonist and the beginning of the development of the book.

CHAPTER 3 — MEET PRESIDENT VONBRAUN

In this chapter, we are privy to the thoughts of BJ vonBraun, the president of the university where Professor Rick teaches. She is talking with colleagues from other universities. Business school registrations are down and they speculate about possible reasons why. Is it because the universities are oversupplying the market? Is it because the word is out that an MBA degree no longer guarantees a lucrative job?

COMMENTARY — CHAPTER 3

The problem of declining registrations at university MBA programs is introduced and possible explanations are proposed. Just like any other enterprise, universities sometimes need more customers.

GLOSSARY — CHAPTER 3

MBA — Master of Business Administration, a post-graduate degree previously, especially in the 90s, considered mandatory for obtaining a management level job with many companies, predominantly, large companies.

CHAPTER 4 - THE PROBLEM WITH PROJECTS

Professor Rick's open discussion style is definitely appealing to his project management students. A few minutes into the first lecture, the professor's class is actively discussing why the train tunnels under the channel between England and France were completed late and over budget, thereby displaying the two classic symptoms of a poorly managed project. Then, they move on to talk about the four oil rig platforms in the North Sea and the less-than-competent planning that went into those particular projects.

Mark, the Genemodem think tank group leader, acknowledges that the project he is working on is in danger of running late and going over budget. The professor asks him what he'll do. Mark admits he'll be forced to change the target specifications for the project, saving some features for a later release. The whole class knows of similar situations. Another student comments that "everybody" knows that when projects finish late or over budget it means compromises were made.

Professor Rick tells them that occasionally there are projects that finish early, under budget, and even provide more than was anticipated. To shore up his claim, the professor recounts the only case in point he knows, that of the U2 spy plane. It's a story of a project that finished way ahead of time. In the 50s when the Russians let it be known that they had the atom bomb, a critical need arose for the United States to find a way to monitor Soviet activities. Although at the time, the customary development time for a new plane was ten years, America had the U2 flying and taking photographs just eight months after project start.

For the next class, Rick gives his students the assignment to select a project at the company for which they work, interview the project leader and bosses of that project, then prepare a list of official reasons for any overruns as well as a list of unofficial reasons.

COMMENTARY – CHAPTER 4

The main point Goldratt is making here is that almost ALL projects fail to meet expectations. Rarely do projects achieve ALL of the objectives set out for them. This means that all projects must suffer from the same type of underlying problem. If we can find this underlying problem and solve it, we can derive a generalized way to approach projects that transcends the project type.

In addition, we find another reference to "open discussion style." This style is the hallmark of the Socratic approach, using questions to cause the students (and you) to think. Eli Goldratt likes this method of teaching and believes it is superior to the Aristotelian method of explaining and giving facts. He uses the classroom setting to tell you what you need to know. This device allows him to assume the role of a Socratic teacher, setting up the questions you should be asking, and then allowing the students to answer. Working through the issues presented in **Critical Chain** prompts readers to think about the problems in new ways.

Additional discussion on project performance can be found in the Reference section.

CHAPTER 5 – BUSINESS SCHOOL ENROLLMENTS ARE DECLINING

President vonBraun is talking with the dean of the university's business school. She is concerned about sagging enrollments and draws a parallel between the declining enrollment in schools of agriculture and what she sees on the horizon for business schools. The dean disagrees. He says that unlike business where you must have an MBA to get to the top, a special degree is not necessary for success if your field is agriculture. VonBraun brings up declining enrollment at law schools and how it now appears that the market for lawyers has been over-satisfied. Her worry is that if enrollment continues to go down, the business school will not be able to carry its own weight financially. Moreover, it will be hard to shrink it down to a supportable size. They agree more information is needed in order to formulate a sound opinion, and that one of the most important areas to research is the probability of graduates landing good jobs within their chosen fields.

COMMENTARY – CHAPTER 5

A hypothesis for the cause of declining enrollments is given: the market for MBA degrees is saturated. How can we see if this true? If the market is saturated, then the graduates will have a difficult time finding jobs that require the MBA. The educators in the story don't know whether or not this is the case, so they need to check. At the time the book was written, this seemed to be the case.

Goldratt is demonstrating one of the thinking tools of the Theory of Constraints (ToC[1]) — effect-cause-effect — that analyzes a system using a scientific method. We have a problem. We hypothesize a cause. If the cause exists in reality, there are other effects we can predict. If we find them, our hypothesis is strengthened.

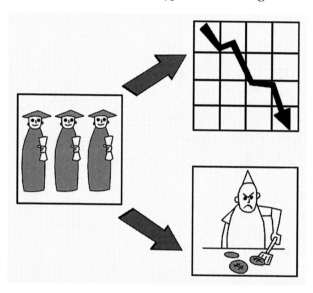

The starting effect is declining enrollments. The speculated cause is market saturation. The predicted effect is that MBAs have a hard time finding a job. Does it exist? We don't know yet.

GLOSSARY – CHAPTER 5

Effect-cause-effect — "A validation method to prove the existence of an underlying cause. When a possible entity is

---

proposed as the cause for an indicated effect, the existence of an additional effect proves the existence of the cause. That is, by showing that the second effect exists, the existence of the common cause is supported." — ToC-ICO Dictionary

Hypothesis — A supposition or assumption; an unproven theory.

Theory of Constraints — A holistic management philosophy developed by Dr. Eliyahu M. Goldratt that is based on the principle that complex systems exhibit inherent simplicity, i.e., even a very complex system made up of thousands of people and pieces of equipment can have any given time only a very, very small number of variables – perhaps only one (know as a constraint) – that actually limits the system's ability to generate more of the system's goal.
Syn: constraint management.

CHAPTER 6 – PROJECTS ARE INHERENTLY UNCERTAIN

Goldratt takes us to the next Executive MBA Program project management class. Professor Rick goes over the results of the last class assignment. Fred, of the Genemodem think tank team, offers that due to budget overruns and production delays, the projected payback time for the project he researched at his company has been moved out from three years to five years. The professor explains, for the benefit of those in the class who may not know, that payback can be defined as the point at which the cost of the project will be recovered. The students identify many reasons — both official and unofficial — for overruns of time and budget. While official reasons for falling short often name the external world (weather conditions, unforeseen difficulties, etc.), unofficial reasons (usually presented by workers closer to the project's detail level) point at internal factors. The class concludes that a better way to manage projects must be found or developed.

After the class spends some time discussing the possibility of adding more supervisors to keep a project on track, the professor helps them see that taking that approach adds consequentially to the problem of synchronization.

It is agreed that the inability to accurately forecast uncertainties is at the root of all missed estimates and the class also concludes that safety must be inserted at each step of a project, not just slapped into the project as a whole. But how much safety time is enough?

Rick introduces his class to the Gaussian Bell Curve of Probability and shows that at the median, there is only a 50% chance of finishing at or before a given time. The students resolve that Murphy's Law is a mitigating factor and agree that while a 50% chance of hitting a targeted estimate is not enough, an 80% to 90% chance is acceptable. There is also a discussion of how people who use their worst experiences as the basis for their estimates create a "self-fulfilling prophecy" of time-eating problems. It is suggested that therefore, as more and more safety is added in hopes of assuring an accurate time line, the more the project expands and actually has a smaller and smaller chance of finishing on schedule.

Professor Rick explains the next homework assignment: to choose three steps from the same company project the students used for their last assignment and find out how the time estimate was calculated for those steps.

The Genemodem think tank trio talks among themselves and determines that they are on to something but need more data in order to accurately understand the role of "self-fulfilling prophecy."

COMMENTARY – CHAPTER 6

The very nature of projects is that they are uncertain. Uncertainty exists in the scope of work required to accomplish the project, the length of time it takes to accomplish each task within a project, and of course, "Murphy" lives in projects, just as he lives in other areas. Our inability to manage uncertainty is the core problem of poor project performance. This is the heart of the solution, the point of attack on the problem.

We are introduced to the concept of uncertainty and probability in task estimations. All task estimates are a probability estimate (and have uncertain outcomes). Projects typically account for this uncertainty at the individual task level. How much allowance for uncertainty exists? Plenty. The text and our experience shows that task time estimates are typically made in the range of 80% to 90% confidence. People have a good reason to be conservative in their estimates because of their experience with organizational pressure. While the project is being executed, a great deal of emphasis is placed on achieving the due date of the task. When the sheep are late coming in from the pasture, the shepherd is held accountable. Shepherds don't like to be hit with their own crooks, so they give conservative estimates to allow the very last, fattest, oldest, slowest sheep to meander back from the pasture.

This is the "Bell Shaped Curve," the Gaussian distribution. If our task estimates had this sort of probability distribution, most of the tasks would finish between 44 days and 46. Half of the tasks would finish before 45 days and half after 45 days. 90% of the time, we would finish in around 47 days.

Goldratt is pointing out in this chapter that our task estimates are not entirely the estimate of the work to be done — the technical limit. There is a significant amount of padding going on, increasing the planned length of the project.. Most of it is legitimate, given that we hit our shepherds with their crooks when they give us unreliable estimates

If there is so much padding going on, why are most projects late?

GLOSSARY – CHAPTER 6

Effect — "An entity representing the result of one or more causes." —ToC-ICO Dictionary

Estimate — An approximate calculation; an opinion or judgment.

Gaussian Curve — In mathematical statistics, the symmetrical bell-shaped graph of a normal distribution.

Murphy — Refers to Murphy's Law. In 1949 a U.S. engineer named E.A. Murphy, Jr. formulated the original version which stated that if there is a possibility for something to go wrong, it will go wrong.

Probability — Likelihood. In math, the ratio of the number of times something will probably occur to the total number of possible occurrences.

Self-fulfilling Prophecy — Conjecture that is brought to fulfillment chiefly as an effect of it having been expected or predicted.

Task — The smallest unit of work in the project, usually performed by a single resource.

Technical Limit — A precise parameter defining where something ceases to be possible; having to do with the practical, industrial, mechanical arts or the applied sciences.

Uncertainty — Doubt that implies a lack of conviction such as through the absence of sufficient evidence.

CHAPTER 7 – DECLINING ENROLLMENTS ARE CAUSED BY CUSTOMER DISSATISFACTION?

VonBraun begins to understand that the business school isn't over-supplying the market with MBAs and that something else is wrong — that the school is not satisfying the market's needs. She wonders if adding value to the program will solve the problem she has uncovered: that an MBA degree has lost relevance. She seeks the counsel of another university president within her circle to explore her idea.

COMMENTARY – CHAPTER 7

Goldratt continues to take us through his example of the effect-cause-effect method. Suppose you make a hypothesis and it turns out to be wrong. How do you know? When you can't find the predicted effect, your hypothesis is invalidated. You must then find a new one and test it.

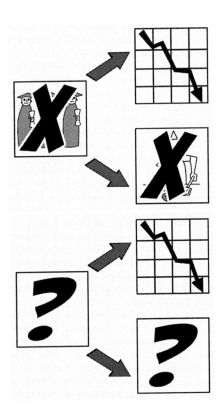

VonBraun's predicted effect does not appear. MBAs don't seem to have any trouble finding jobs. Thus, the original hypothesis is probably not correct. What else could be the reason? Could it be that the MBA has lost its relevance? Is there no longer much perceived value in having an MBA? What is the predicted effect? How could we know? President vonBraun doesn't either. So, she asks for help.

CHAPTER 8 – PROJECT MANAGERS LOSE SIGHT OF THE OBJECTIVE

Professor Rick and Jim, his department head, meet. The deal they have made is that the professor will do the heavy lifting in the research and writing of a series of articles about project management. As department head, Jim's name will appear first on their collaborative effort. Professor Rick has been lax about publishing, something he must do in order to advance beyond associate professor status at the university. He, therefore, has a vested interest in completing these articles.

The pair is trying to zero in on substantive subject matter for their first article and Jim is excited by information that has emerged from Rick's work with his class. It appears that the lower down on the corporate ladder a manager is, the more he is willing to point a finger of blame inside the company, not just at external factors. It also appears that while most people think so, spending too much money is not the most important negative financial implication. As Rick and Jim continue to talk, it becomes obvious that companies with a "saving mindset" often forget that the goal of a project is to make money, not just conserve it. It also becomes obvious that the "real world" homework assignments done by the Executive MBA students will provide the foundation upon which these two educators will base their articles.

COMMENTARY – CHAPTER 8

Rick's underlying idea is that while most projects are justified based on significantly increasing value to the organization, once the project is launched, the project team loses sight of the objective of the project and focuses more effort on saving resources (maintaining budget). This behavior points to another problem in projects, the lack of a good economic decision model that everyone in the project can use to make good decisions. Without the ability to make informed trade-offs between project costs and benefits, managers are forced to pay attention to the one "concrete" item they can grasp; the project budget.

CHAPTER 9 – HOW TO MANAGE THE PROJECT?

Back in his classroom again, Professor Rick leads the class through a review of PERT and the Critical Path technique. Using an example of a project to build a working factory, he defines the critical path as the longest chain of dependent tasks. Rick stresses that if there is a delay along the critical path, it will be reflected as a delay in the completion of the project. Two Gantt charts are drawn and a student defines an early start date for one while another student defines a delayed start date for the other. A debate ensues about whether, if the late start date is specified, the financial advantage gained from postponing investment in the new facility will outweigh the risk to the finish date. Then, the argument is presented that when one starts all paths at their earliest possible start date, this could easily create delay by causing the project leader to lose focus. It is also observed that the financial penalty for delaying potential income from the project almost always overshadows every other consideration.

A student states what's become obvious: a better way to manage projects needs to be found. This leads to a discussion of how to measure project progress. A "control mechanism" is defined as a way to measure progress, but that definition of control falls short. Activity reports aren't generated until after a problem has done its damage. Professor Rick points out that any way of measuring that doesn't take the critical path into consideration doesn't contribute timely information — the critical path and *only* the critical path establishes the project finish date. Delays on the critical path will translate to delays in finishing the project.

COMMENTARY – CHAPTER 9

There are three important concepts being introduced here:

1. Critical Path

2. Starting early or late on non-critical paths

3. Defining the meaning of "Control"

Critical Path

Goldratt is pointing us to the idea that there is a "critical" sequence of tasks that determine the overall lead-time of the project. The corollary to this is that tasks *not* on the critical path do not affect the project lead-time or completion date.

In this example, the longest sequence of activities is A (6 days), C^2 (6 days), D (3 days). The total duration of this project should be 15 days. This sequence defines the duration of the project.

STARTING EARLY

While it's commonly accepted that the critical path determines the length of the project, there is a widespread behavior in projects of starting all tasks possible as soon as the project is released, even if those tasks are on non-critical paths. In the example above, most project managers would initiate work on C^1, A, and B simultaneously, even though only A is on the critical path and the other tasks are not "due" yet.

There are two main effects of starting tasks too early. Starting tasks early causes the organization to invest earlier than what is "strictly" required, increasing expenses and the risk of rework in the project. However, the author points us to another, more significant ramification, losing focus, which could cause the project manager to "miss" something important in the project, thereby delaying the project completion date. Contrary to popular belief, starting early does not mean finishing early. It means finishing *later*.

This points to another problem: that project managers have nothing to guide them in determining where to focus. Goldratt is offering a different definition of "control." Control is not responding after a problem has done its damage; control is finding areas of risk and responding *before* the project due date is affected. Every project manager knows that deciding when to respond to a "problem" is an issue. Is EVERY delay in a project something to be managed? For many project managers, the answer is yes. Experienced project managers realize that if they respond to every task delay, they will not have a life. Goldratt has already established the task times are estimated conservatively, so project managers know intuitively that time lost on a single task can be "made up" on a subsequent task. Yet, many projects are managed as through EVERY task's due date was essential to the project's success. In this behavior, we see a negative reinforcing loop. People give conservative task estimates. People miss the date because things go wrong. We beat them up. Next time, we get an even more conservative estimate of task duration from them. Give me that crook!

Still, the issue remains. How should the project manager focus?

GLOSSARY – CHAPTER 9

Critical Path — The longest set of dependent activities within a project.

Control — "A reactive mechanism to handle uncertainty by monitoring information that can point to a threatening situation and preparing corrective actions accordingly." —Eli Schragenheim

Gantt Chart — "A graphic representation of the duration of tasks against the progression of time." —www.ganttchart.com, Retrieved September 10, 2005.

PERT — Program Evaluation and Review Technique. A system of planning, scheduling, controlling, and reviewing a series of interdependent events in order to follow a proper sequence and complete a project as quickly and inexpensively as possible. —Webster's New World Dictionary (1984) p1008, New York, NY, Simon & Schuster

CHAPTER 10 – START EARLY OR AS LATE AS POSSIBLE?

In this chapter, we catch up with Professor Rick who must publish articles in order to move from associate to full professor. Rick is meeting with Jim, his department head, and we see that he is getting a lesson in the finer points of the "publish or perish" aspect of university teaching. Rick tells Jim that he has a new idea for a first collaborative article. It is about the problem of early start versus late start. Jim comments that untold numbers of articles have already been written on the subject of optimization. Rick is not discouraged — he is coming at this from a new angle and thinks the ideas set forth in previously published articles failed to hone in on the major issue: the ability of the project manager to focus. He claims that both early start and late start jeopardize the ability to focus, although to varying degrees. Jim, although he would like to find a breakthrough (like Just-In-Time or TQM) significant enough to be accepted even though it was based on logic and not a math, sees a problem with that approach to the article. Academic reviewers still demand articles based on surveys or mathematical models. Articles based on common sense or logical procedures simply won't pass scrutiny.

Rick also has an idea for a second article but it is equally unable to meet the publishing criteria. His assertion is that the accepted way project progress is measured is wrong and that instead, measurements should be used to encourage each component to perform in a way that benefits the entire system.

COMMENTARY – CHAPTER 10

Goldratt, as is his habit, is once again challenging the status quo. He uses his characters to pose the question, "Which is more valid, studies or logic?" Most research depends on surveys and algorithms, not process. Very few academics ask how to put their research to practical use. "Practical" research is left in the hands of consultants.

Goldratt also points to measurements as being part of the critical chain solution. In many projects, progress is measured incorrectly, leading project managers to a false sense of security of the progress of the project, only to discover , too late, that their project is in trouble.

GLOSSARY – CHAPTER 10

Just-In-Time (JIT) — A system that does not stockpile raw materials ahead of time and depends on receiving materials and components on a "just in time" as needed basis.

"Publish or perish" — an expression that refers to the well known preference of universities to only reward professors who have developed and published course-related concepts.

TQM —Total Quality Management

CHAPTER II - THE THEORY OF CONSTRAINTS AND PROJECT MANAGEMENT

In this chapter, Professor Rick attends a colloquium given by Johnny Fisher, an MBA program professorial associate who has just returned from a year's sabbatical spent working at UniCo. UniCo, a company known for expansion and profits, is using the Theory of Constraints (ToC). Johnny explains ToC as an innovative management philosophy that introduces new methods and boasts a wide variety of applications. Simply stated, ToC is how to win against the competition.

A top manager in the audience asks about a specific problem he is having — how to shrink development time. Johnny responds that using a ToC approach will solve that "symptom" and others by solving the core problem. Managers must, Johnny says, simultaneously control costs while protecting throughput. He identifies those two actions as two "necessary conditions" but later explains that the "cost world" way of doing things is not always in harmony with the "throughput world" way of doing things. Then, he uses an analogy about links in a chain to re-emphasize what he's said about controlling costs and hammers it home. Johnny makes the point that current convention dictates a "cost world" style management view that asserts that local improvements improve the organization as a whole; that global improvement is accomplished by making many local improvements.

Next, Johnny surprises his audience by explaining that "protecting throughput" is contradictory to the way almost every manager runs his organization.. He uses the label "throughput world" to describe the opposite of common practice and then revisits his link analogy. Johnny explains that if one link represents each department (purchasing, production, finishing, assembly, shipping, etc.), if there is a failure in any one area, the throughput of the entire company will be negatively affected. Linkages, he says, are also important. If even only one link breaks, the chain is broken and as a single entity, it no longer has any strength at all.

Johnny asks what determines the strength of the chain. The weakest link is the answer, and at any given time, there can only be one. Johnny then tells the group that while most local improvements do not result in corporate-wide benefit and since they require attention, time and money, they do not strengthen the total organization. Therefore, most local improvements are directed towards the stronger links in the chain.

The subject switches momentarily to the Pareto Principle as a prelude to proving that there can be no compromise between cost-driven and throughput-driven management styles. The Pareto Principle applied to problem solving requires limiting the focus to only what is most important. It states that if you solve the most important 20% of what is wrong, you'll reap 80% of the benefits you would get by solving all of the problems. It works, however, only when applied to situations where the variables are independent, so, continues Johnny, it can only be successfully applied in "cost world" situations where each variable (link) is managed separately.

Johnny then tells the group that what is needed first is to find the weakest link or, to say it another way, IDENTIFY the system's constraint. If it's physical, such as a bottleneck, strengthening the weakest link will help the bottleneck produce more. If it's a policy constraint, replacing the erroneous policy will correct the problem. The next step, says Johnny, is to EXPLOIT the system's constraint by increasing capacity or squeezing the maximum out of it and then examining the ramifications of what you've done to linked processes. Third, he continues, SUBORDINATE everything else you do to your bottleneck decision. If you can only produce X units an hour at the bottleneck, it is pointless to produce more at non-bottleneck locations. Next, Johnny tells the group, ELEVATE the system's constraint. You accomplish that, he explains, by adding capacity to get more throughput if necessary. Lastly, REPEAT. Go back to IDENTIFY and start again. Why? Because, Johnny tells them, the constraint originally identified is no longer the weakest link. The weakest link is now elsewhere. These five steps, Johnny concludes, provide the focus needed to instill ongoing improvement in the organization as a whole.

Johnny has already indicated that there is no acceptable compromise between the "cost world" and the "throughput world." He gives an example to illustrate what happens when the corporate culture continues to measure success by measuring local performance efficiency even though the goal is increasing organizational throughput. Slowing down the production on non-bottlenecks to keep pace with the bottleneck will result in serious consequences for non-bottleneck managers who will be seen as lagging in efficiency.

He points out that while it is accepted that the first step in problem solving is precise definition of the problem, we can't know if we've defined it precisely until we have solved it. ToC, however, uses the definition accepted in the hard sciences, "A problem is not considered precisely defined until it can be presented as a conflict between two necessary conditions." So, what's the solution? Johnny Fisher uses the example of trying to measure the height of a building. If two different answers are found by using two different systems of measurement, the hard sciences would dictate that there is no room for compromise. Rather, says Johnny, we recognize that one or more faulty assumptions (stemming from using one style of measuring or the other or both) are present and must be corrected. By correcting the faulty assumption, the conflict is removed. ToC uses a tool called an "evaporating cloud," Johnny explains. It is used to expose hidden assumptions and challenge them so unsatisfactory methods and compromises can be replaced with win-win solutions.

He sums up by saying that one accepting the conventional thinking that good cost performance can only be achieved through good across-the-board local performance is regarded as the root problem of many organizations.

COMMENTARY – CHAPTER II

UniCo is the same company discussed in Goldratt's first book, **The Goal**.

In this chapter, Goldratt is explaining that ToC is much more than managing bottlenecks. ToC should be viewed more as a way to manage and improve the enterprise; which is analogous to a chain. The first priority of ToC is to improve the overall health of the company.

IMPROVEMENT EVERYWHERE VERSUS FOCUSED IMPROVEMENTS

In discussing the necessary conditions of ToC, we see that two of them are controlling costs and protecting throughput. In other words, managers should guard against overspending and also guard the throughput capabilities of the business, two seemingly conflicting goals. However, neither should be the main objective of a manager — he should be focusing on the weak link in the chain in order to improve the overall performance of the enterprise.

Goldratt also introduces the concept of dependent versus independent links; an important distinction. When there is no *dependence*, the Pareto principle of 20:80 (actions to benefits) is valid. When there are dependent relationships among the tasks and resources, as we find in the chain analogy, the relationship of action-to-benefit changes to more of a 1:99 ratio.

In the graph below, this difference is illustrated. Pareto's law is expressed as the darker line.

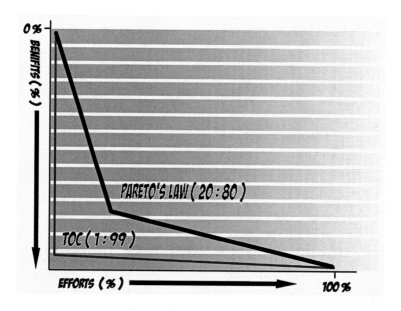

PROBLEMS ARE CONFLICTS

Goldratt explains the underlying thinking behind the evaporating cloud technique of problem solving — expressing problems as conflicts rather than choosing a compromise solution. The technique helps identify the underlying assumptions that lead to the conflict as well as the ones that are erroneous.

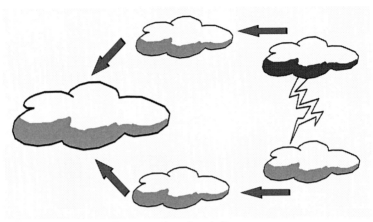
Evaporating cloud diagram

Additional discussion on the Theory of Constraints can be found in the Reference section.

GLOSSARY – CHAPTER II

Bottleneck — any resource with capacity equal to or less than the demand placed upon it.

Cost World — "A paradigm primarily concerned with "saving" money. The view that a system consists of a series of independent variables; each being an independent cost driver; the unavoidable conclusion is that the way to judge actions and decisions is by their local impact, and in order to quantify local impact cost allocation must be used." —ToC-ICO Dictionary

Core Conflict — The systemic conflict that causes the vast majority of the UDEs (Undesirable Effects) in the CRT (Current Reality Tree). The conflict appears between two opposing entities that are prerequisites for two necessary conditions for satisfying the systemic goal.

Evaporating Cloud — A visual representation used to expose hidden assumptions and challenge them so unsatisfactory methods and compromises can be replaced with win-win solutions.

Pareto's Law — Refers to the 80:20 rule of unequal distribution in which a small proportion of causes produce a large proportion of results. Pareto was an economist and sociologist who lived from 1848-1923.

System Constraint — The weakest link. Can be physical such as a bottleneck or nonphysical such as an erroneous policy.

Throughput World — "A paradigm primarily concerned with "making" money. The view that a system consists of a series of dependent variables that must work together to achieve the goal and whose ability to do so is limited by some system constraint; the unavoidable conclusion that the global improvement is the direct result of improvement at the constraint, and cost allocation is totally unnecessary and misleading. This paradigm is in contrast with the 'cost world' paradigm." —ToC-ICO Dictionary

CHAPTER 12 – ERRONEOUS MEASUREMENTS CREATE ERRONEOUS BEHAVIORS

After a break, Johnny moves his presentation back to a discussion of his hands-on experience at UniCo. UniCo purchased a steel company and Don Pederson, an especially powerful VP, asked Johnny to conduct an in-depth analysis of it. Johnny found that the steel company was losing money, like so many other companies in that industry. On the plus side, delivery, due-date performance and pricing were as good as the competitors, and quality was a little better. The technology was fine and most equipment was completely up to date. A number of machines would need to be replaced, but that could be accomplished with a payback of just three years. On the down side, inventory was stacking up, the computer system used for planning was ancient in technology terms, and the company was spending more on raw materials than necessary.

Johnny Fisher was ready to present all his findings and recommendations to Pederson, but the VP only wanted to know what the constraint was. So, Johnny presented his list of 26 constraints. Then, the VP wanted to know how long it was going to take for the company to become profitable. Johnny didn't have an answer, but he did know exactly how much money would be required to invest in the company. Pederson, however, didn't seem interested.

The following day, Don Pederson and Johnny (who was there at UniCo on a grant paid for by UniCo) sat down with 20 top managers of the newly acquired company. Pederson said he understood that tons-per-hour was the prime measurement used by the steel industry and he asked if the managers thought they were doing a good job monitoring tons-per-hour. They felt they were. Then, he threw them a curve. He asked if they *should* be monitoring tons per hour. Their responses revealed they had not considered this question. The measurement was simply part of their culture.

Pederson reminded them that an operational measurement's primary purpose is to encourage departments to serve not just themselves, but also the company as a whole. He put up a chart, a Current Reality Tree (CRT), analyzing the steel producer and started reading it. Then, beginning with the core statement that tons-per-hour was the prime measurement in the steel industry, Pederson led the managers through "branch" after "branch" of current realities in their business until he was able to conclude with what the uppermost box said, "To maximize their performance of tons-per-hour, departments tend to take actions that result in 'stealing.'"

The managers, under Don Pederson's guidance, started making estimates of the impact a tons-per-hour measurement had on their company. They identified lost sales, excess inventory, wasted cost, long delivery lead ties, unreliable due-date performance, and time wasted in arguments among departments. Don asked about other problems. As they raised each new problem, he asked them to calculate the negative impact. Among other unexpected realizations, they also came to understand that if extra inventory was not produced in such large quantities, they would have more raw materials on hand; if lead times were much shorter, clients wouldn't have time to change their minds.

Pederson, the UniCo VP, helped the steel company managers see and agree that the root problem, the constraint, was using tons-per-hour as their prime operational measurement. He explained that correcting how they measured could give the company a tremendous edge that would last as long as competitors still measured tons-per-hour.

Wrapping up the story of his time with Don Pederson, Johnny Fisher reiterated to his university audience that the steel industry was committed to using tons-per-hour because their management philosophies were based on the "cost world" and not the "throughput world." Consequently, the only way they could achieve good cost performance was by having good local performance everywhere.

Johnny said he was embarrassed about giving the UniCo VP a list of more than 20 constraints — that he now knew that in real life systems there are no more than one or perhaps two constraints. Of course, back at the time when he developed his long list, Johnny still had a lot to learn. He was just beginning to understand the Theory of Constraints and he'd never before seen a Current Reality Tree.

Johnny said that the cause and effect thinking process of ToC that is known as an evaporating cloud (a way of visually presenting the problem as a conflict between two necessary conditions) caused a revolution in his work — that by refusing to look for a compromise (or to "optimize," as academia calls it), and to instead expose the underlying assumptions, an actual solution can be found. He confessed that he stopped fiddling with symptoms entirely and completed another paradigm shift once he was introduced to the Current Reality Tree.

COMMENTARY - CHAPTER 12

Goldratt is demonstrating the two premises of ToC he introduced earlier in the book. He doesn't name the company in **Critical Chain**, but during his live lectures he often refers to the ToC analysis in this chapter as the "Bethlehem Steel case study."

By presenting the Current Reality Tree (CRT), Goldratt is demonstrating the practicality and power of one of the ToC tools.

It's another premise of ToC that the only problems worth working on are core problems. These are the problems that explain the most undesirable effects in a system.

THE premise of ToC stresses that the performance of any system is determined by few variables — the constraint(s). Any system will have VERY few of these.

Another principle asserts that many undesirable effects can be linked to each other and to a single root cause using cause and effect thinking.

There is an analogy here; in steel manufacturing, resources "steal" material from one job to work on another, moving capacity into inventory that cannot be immediately used for sales. This causes other problems, as that capacity was needed for other orders, creating additional expediting and confusion in the plant. Isn't it true, in some project environments, that we measure resources in similar terms? Encouraging them to focus on their personal or local department's performance? Don't you see similar effects? Lost sales? Late deliveries? Expediting? Excessive work in process? Arguments about resource allocation?

The main point here is that having the wrong local performance measurements can create behaviors that actually lead to damaging the ability of the organization to compete.

GLOSSARY – CHAPTER 12

Current Reality Tree — A diagram that begins with a core statement about a given business, shows pertinent realities, and ends with a conclusion. A logic-based tool hat uses cause-and-effect relationships to link root problems to the resulting undesirable system effects (UDEs).

CHAPTER 13 – WHY PROJECTS TAKE TOO LONG

Back at the Executive MBA program class for project management, the students were to have completed their assignments documenting why employees at various levels in their companies build safety time into their projects. There is, however, only one paper turned in and it appears that nobody has any real answers because the students all had trouble getting anyone at their companies to admit that safety time was actually being added to estimates.

Professor Rick probes. The class finally realizes that they really do have the answer after all. It is revealed that the vast majority of employees expect they have at least an 80% chance of finishing on time as long as they are 1) not delayed by others or 2) loaded up with too much else to do. They also discover that the boss adds his own safety time cushion on top of theirs. When numerous layers of management are involved, each layer adds more safety time. Then, top management makes a global cut in the projected time it will take for the entire project to finish — a cut that managers had already padded their estimates to absorb. Professor Rick concludes that there are at least three reasons excessive safety is added to time estimates:

1. Estimates are influenced by previous negative experiences.

2. The more layers of management there are, the bigger the final estimate will be.

3. Global cuts are anticipated, so time estimates are increased to absorb them.

The professor also concludes that safety time makes up the lion's share of the estimated time it will take to complete a project. The class then determines that delays that occur during one step get passed on to the next step, but the converse is not true — extra progress made during a step is rarely passed along. So, delays accumulate but advances do not. Professor Rick equates guarding the performance of each step to "cost world" philosophy while he equates acknowledging the performance of the project as a whole to "throughput world" philosophy..

One class member attributes "wasted safety" to "students' syndrome." Another says it is "bad multitasking" that impacts negatively by inflating lead times and wasting set up time. Self-fulfilling prophecy is mentioned as a negative contributor, too, because if one thinks a project will take longer, the project will expand to fill the time allotted. Concern that there will be times when people are not working steadily and efficiencies may drop (especially when dependencies between steps are involved) also plays a role.

For the next class session, Rick asks his students to be ready with an example for each of the three devices that people use to increase safety and three for the devices that waste it.

COMMENTARY – CHAPTER 13

In spite of the fact that task durations are often conservatively estimated to begin with, the presence of certain behaviors can cause them to increase even more. Three important behaviors make project durations longer than necessary. They are:

DELIBERATE PADDING

Once the people doing the work have conservatively estimated their tasks, the estimates are then passed through several layers of management where they are increased even more. Because managers feel they must protect their own performance, in many organizations task estimates are not treated as "estimates," they are treated as "commitments." People don't want to be late on commitments, thus, they "pad" their estimates of how long a given task will take.

STUDENT SYNDROME

"Student syndrome" is a term that pertains to the psychology of procrastinating, something students are particularly prone to do. The analogy is to students who are going to take a test. When do they study for it? The night before! Why? Because they have much more important things to do! Often in projects, people start too late, using their safety time to work on other things, thinking they still have enough time to complete the task on time. After they begin the task, they run into problems, causing it to take even longer than the original padded estimate. The student syndrome causes longer durations because some of the time needed to complete a task is lost when it's started too late or even when it's started "just in time." Then, Murphy causes the task to take even longer.

This "Murphy" is really two things: common cause process variation and special cause process variation. The two types of variation are not differentiated in the text, but in the implementation, must be treated differently. Common cause variation can be predicted and managed using the CCPM approach. Special cause variation must be treated separately in a risk analysis process.

BAD MULTITASKING

Multitasking occurs when an individual is working on more than one task at the same time. There are two kinds of multitasking: good and bad. Good multitasking is moving two or more tasks along together smoothly, such as catching up on customer calls while heading to a meeting. On the other hand, bad multitasking is anything but smooth. It's the dropping of work on one task before it is finished in order to start another, only to stop and begin yet another task or go back to a previous task. All too often, people aren't able to complete a task without getting pulled off onto something else, so "task time" grows each time a change is necessary. Goldratt wants you to see that the majority of task completion time is not used for the actual work, but is waiting or queue time. Tasks ready to be worked on cannot be worked on because there is no available resource. If the estimates are too long, during execution the actual time will grow even longer! No wonder projects consistently finish late and over budget.

PARKINSON'S LAW

Parkinson's Law states the amount of work rises to fill the time available to complete it. In projects, it means that early task completions are never reported. Resources will continue to work on "improving" their task or will simply find something else to do until the due date of that task. In any case, the result to the project is that only the late finishes are recognized, so the only way a project timeline moves is out.

These two behaviors, student syndrome and multi-tasking, have the same root cause — the lack of clear priorities. Student syndrome occurs when you believe the real due date is distant relative to the amount of time needed to complete the task, while bad multitasking is caused by not recognizing the real priority of tasks until they become late relative to the "need by" date.

WHY DO PROJECTS TAKE SO LONG?

1. We add too much time to the original plan. We allow x amount of time, so it takes x amount of time.

2. Our resources multi-task, adding unnecessary work (additional setups) to the project

3. The Student Syndrome causes us to waste whatever buffer we *did* have, adding more time to our already generous estimates.

4. Parkinson's Law blocks us from taking advantage of any favorable variation (tasks finishing early) the project experiences.

IMPLICATIONS FOR MANAGEMENT

Critical chain seeks to reduce / eliminate these behaviors, and therefore they are not planned for in the project. We can overcome deliberate padding, student syndrome, bad multitasking and Parkinson's Law through better management and communication.

If we can eliminate these behaviors from our projects, the time to finish the project is reduced. For example, looking at our project with the critical path (A, C², & D), you see the length of the path is 15 days.

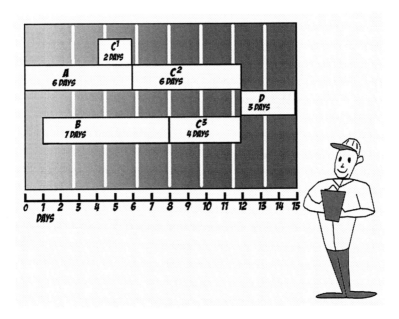

After removing the safety time from these tasks, the critical path is shortened significantly, to 8 days. This is one of the reasons that critical chain projects consistently finish in less time than projects that do not use this approach.

GLOSSARY – CHAPTER 13

Bad Multitasking — The dropping of work on one task before it is finished in order to start another.

Common Cause Variation — a source of variation caused by unknown factors that result in a steady but random distribution of output around the average or mean of the data

Special Cause Variation — variation caused by known factors that result in a non-random distribution of output; also referred to as "exceptional" or "assignable" variation.

Parkinson's Law — The satirical statement that work expands to fill the time allotted to it expressed as a law by a British economist in the early 1900s.

Students' Syndrome — The type of procrastination students are prone to when they are assigned a project or are facing a test.

CHAPTER 14 - INCREASING THROUGHPUT IS THE MAIN GOAL

Professor Rick is turned down for tenure and all teaching extensions have been eliminated. Effectively, he is out the door — there are no exceptions. A freeze is on for all university financial commitments. The professor calls everybody he knows. Nobody wants a business teacher. He demands to see the president of the university. She stonewalls him until he asks her if it will make a difference if he is able to bring more students into the Executive MBA program. In desperation, he tells her he can get them to enroll because he teaches project management and projects are where the money is. He informs her that he can infuse the program with valuable new know-how. She tells him to prove it first by actually bringing 10 new students in and if he does, she'll extend his teaching contract one more year.

COMMENTARY - CHAPTER 14

In this very short chapter, Goldratt is making three points:

1. There is more than one way to respond when sales are down.

2. Projects are economically significant.

3. Business schools can compete based on providing useful knowledge to industry.

Increasing throughput is a theme present throughout Goldratt's books. When you have a reduction in sales, your first response should not be to reduce expenses, but instead to find a way to increase demand by challenging your perception of what the market really wants. This is counter to the approach of many managers, where their first reaction to a drop in sales is to slash budgets. By telling us about the university, Goldratt hopes his readers will see that there is an alternative to making devastating layoffs when sales decline.

The view of ToC is that expenses are only cut as a last resort. The first response when sales are declining should be to examine assumptions about the company's offer in terms of the real value it provides to the market. The company's "offer" consists of every aspect that touches the customer: the product, support, delivery lead time, reliability, and financial terms. In questioning your company's offer and the market's requirements, you may discover a need that has been overlooked.

Goldratt is using the university's business program to challenge your thinking about your offer. What is it? What value does it bring? Who is the customer? In many cases, the students in MBA programs do not pay for their classes; their employers do. Who benefits most from the program? Certainly the students benefit, however, the students are not the primary beneficiaries. The employers are. The challenge is to not get confused about who the customer is. Who derives the most benefit from your company's offer? You are challenged to question your own assumptions about who YOUR customer is.

Projects are the lifeblood of most organizations; not just project-based organizations such as construction and software companies. Product development is a project. Productivity improvements are projects. Business acquisitions are projects. Market development efforts are projects. Every single strategic component of the enterprise is a project. Thus, the economic health of the organization rests on the organization's ability to conceive, plan and execute projects successfully. Projects are where the money is because of the value to the organization they add.

GLOSSARY – CHAPTER 14

Offer — A company's "offer" consists of what touches the customer: the product, support, delivery lead time, reliability and financial terms.

CHAPTER 15 – PROJECTS ARE SIMILAR TO PRODUCTION

Several of the professors ask for a meeting with Johnny Fisher, the professor who just came back from a sabbatical he spent working at UniCo. It seems that students are bringing up in other classes what they've learned in the production course Johnny teaches. The professors want Johnny to teach them what he's been teaching his students. They say they learned a great deal by attending his colloquium, but need to know more. Specifically, they want to understand the production application of ToC.

Johnny begins taking them through the focusing steps of IDENTIFY, EXPLOIT, SUBORDINATE, ELEVATE and GO BACK. He says the production application is a straight deduction.

To illustrate the first step, identifying the constraint, he draws a line of circles on the board to represent work centers and says the workflow is from left to right. Then, Johnny draws an "X" on one of the middle circles and says that we want to get one hundred percent capacity from that particular work center.

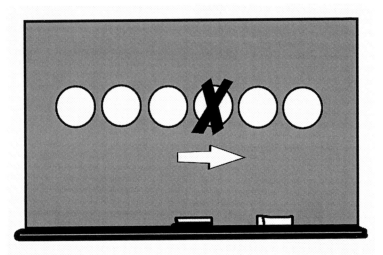

He explains that in order for it not to become a bottleneck, the work centers ahead of it that are feeding it must continually supply enough material. In order to accomplish that, Johnny continues, and simultaneously deal with Murphy's Law and a myriad of other problems that can crop up, the feeding machines must have a lot of excess capacity — enough to accomplish their own work and at the same time, continually replenish the stocks ahead of "X."

Professor Rick is trying to relate what Johnny is saying about production to a project environment. So, he challenges Johnny to convert the five focusing steps to a practical logistical solution. Johnny makes an analogy that leads to the conclusion that work-in-process inventory and lead-time are twin brothers — if work-in-process increases, lead-time will automatically expand and throughput will be lost. Trying to run things more efficiently won't work when there is a bottleneck, says Johnny.

Rick compares manufacturing to projects; saying that the materials waiting at machines in production are what safety time is to projects. They accomplish the same thing; ensuring full utilization of each resource. However, these queues have a downside as well; increasing lead times and the complexity of managing the work. Johnny agrees but says the problem is even more egregious in projects because in production, inventory does not disappear. In projects however, time lost is gone forever.

It becomes clear that the only place one hundred percent efficiency is really needed, the only place protection is really needed, is at the bottleneck. Jim, Professor Rick's department head is also present. He interjects that in order to EXPLOIT the constraint, it must be protected from disruptions elsewhere in the process. Then, Johnny jumps back in with the "how to" explanation: create a buffer. He tells them to get started on choosing the length of the buffer by calculating half of the production lead-time. This buffer then will control when tasks are released into the system, eliminating the early start/late start problem.

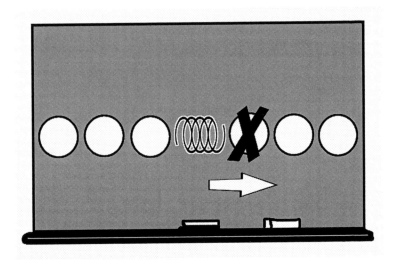

COMMENTARY – CHAPTER 15

Johnny is telling us that trying to run things more efficiently won't work when there is a bottleneck. In other words, you cannot expect to use every resource to 100%. Some resources have extra capacity relative to the bottleneck and thus, will be under-utilized or "inefficient."

To achieve maximum project throughput, you have to focus on the bottleneck. This one resource should be busy 100% of the time working on project tasks. All other resources should be working to enable this resource to achieve this goal. In addition, a time buffer should be introduced to protect the bottleneck, ensuring it is never starved for work.

CHAPTER 16 — DEVELOPING THE CRITICAL CHAIN SOLUTION

The three Genemodem "think tank" members in Professor Rick's project management class invite him to their company to speak to the A226 modem development team. Rick's student trio is keenly aware that they need his help to convince the team of their concepts — they know that without buy-in, there will be no real progress.

Professor Rick pays the Genemodem development team a visit and is able to lead them to a consensus. He summarizes the three points upon which they agree:

1. The common approach is that the finish time (due date) of each step (task) must be protected in order to protect the finish date of the whole project.

2. To accomplish item 1, safety time is added — lots of safety time.

3. There are three reasons for wasted safety time: students' syndrome, multi-tasking and the fact that delays accumulate while advances don't.

The five focusing steps of IDENTIFY, EXPLOIT, SUBORDINATE, ELEVATE and GO BACK are also agreed upon and added to the board. Then, Professor Rick convinces the team to adopt the logical by-product of what appears on the board — a solution that they would now develop together.

Professor Rick wants to know what the constraint on their A226 modem project is, so he asks them to IDENTIFY a bottleneck. The group identifies "production," saying they never have enough of their best products to supply initial market demand. So, Rick defines a bottleneck as a resource lacking adequate capacity to produce enough products to satisfy the market. Then, Rick translates this to the Genemodem development team's current situation. The A226 is now in engineering, so the needed outcome would not yet be quantity, but finishing the development of the modem on or ahead of time.

They look at an existing PERT chart and determine that the constraint, what they select as the equivalent of the bottleneck, is the critical path. Professor Rick guides them in figuring out how to EXPLOIT the constraint — how to harness it as an advantage rather than a problem. They determine that the team must stop fortifying each step in the path with safety time that will be wasted. Instead, that safety time must be put at the end of the path where it will protect the completion date of the project. Removing the safety time earmarked for each individual step, Rick advises, will cut loose enough time to create a "project buffer." He explains that the project buffer will protect the project as a whole.

Next, Rick tells them that in order to do a good job of EX-PLOITING the constraint; they must SUBORDINATE everything else to the constraint. That, he explains, will protect the constraint from problems at non-constraints. A new plan is developed. It depicts time buffers where a feeding path merges with the critical path. The "feeding buffers," says Professor Rick, protect the critical path from delays in the non-critical paths. If a problem causes a delay longer than the time available in the feeding buffer, the project completion date is still protected by the project buffer.

Rick turns his attention to the Genemodem development team's plan and notices how many tasks are marked red as top priorities. Nobody can explain why so many steps are red flagged except to say that these steps must be completed before the following step can happen. For the majority of the flagged steps, the need to expedite does not stand up to close scrutiny, but to ensure delays due to resources that may not be immediately available to work on the critical chain, the team devises the "resource buffer."

COMMENTARY – CHAPTER 16

This chapter is the culmination of the logic presented and we're given a big part of the answer to the problem. We find the premises upon which to build a solution and discover what's wrong with the current approach.

1. Convention that dictates the finish time (due date) of each step must be protected in order to protect the finish date of the whole project.

2. There is quite a bit of unnecessary safety built into task estimates.

3. The safety is then wasted through inappropriate behaviors.

4. The five focusing steps are a valid approach to managing projects, i.e., project management performance is mainly a matter of resource allocation.

Goldratt sketches the **Critical Chain** solution (but not all of it) in the context of three of the five focusing steps.

1. Identify the constraint — the longest sequence of task dependencies. Since we are dealing with a project, a sub-system of the global system, we look for the constraint that prevents us from realizing our goal: the project objectives. We assume the project is worthwhile and will lead the organization closer to its goal.

2. To exploit the constraint, we have to make the critical path as short as possible and ensure we can actually DO it. However, to fully exploit it, there should be no delay from non-critical paths, thus Goldratt moves directly to subordination of (or synchronization to) the critical path.

3. Subordination is achieved by buffering the critical chain from the feeding chains and then synchronizing the feeding chains to the planned dates along the critical path.

BUFFERING

Goldratt discusses the concept of time buffers here as protection for the critical path and the project due date. The feeding buffers protect the critical chain from being disrupted by problems in a non-critical chain. Overall system throughput is thereby protected.

GLOSSARY – CHAPTER 16

Buy-in — The process of committing to a concept or plan.

Feeding Buffer – A time buffer placed between non -Critical Chain work and the Critical Chain. It is used to protect the Critical Chain, the Project Constraint, from variation on non-critical chain paths of work as they feed into the Critical Chain. It is also a factor in determining the start of non-critical chain work.

Project Buffer –A time buffer at the end of the critical chain. Syn: completion buffer.

Resource Buffer - The resource buffer is used to ensure that resources working on a critical chain task or most penetrating chain task are available early if needed. It is merely a warning mechanism. It is sized based on the level of warning that is needed in the environment. This allows us to take advantage of early finishes. It does not add time to the project lead time. (ToC-ICO Dictionary)

SUBORDINATE — The third of the five focusing steps of ToC which requires making everything in the system dependent upon the action of the constraint.

CHAPTER 17 – MANAGING THE PROJECT

The class meets again and the students are aware of Professor Rick's work at Genemodem. They are anxious to know, although he is still very early into the implementation, if there are any definitive results. He tells them that by modifying attitudes and behaviors, a great deal of progress has indeed been made in just three weeks.

Fred, of the Genemodem "think tank" trio, comments that his company has changed how progress is measured. Now, says Fred, progress is measured by finding what percentage of the critical path has been completed.

There is discussion about how changing peoples' attitudes can positively modify behaviors. Mark, the leader of the Genemodem think tank, explains that false alarms are down because managers are no longer pressuring others for work when there's not enough to continually keep their people busy. He also remarks that elimination of false alarms in conjunction with reduction of the time allowed for the performance of steps has helped reduce multitasking. People, he says, are more focused. Ruth, also of the Genemodem team, says abandonment of task due dates has ended the procrastination that stems from "students' syndrome." The third person from Genemodem, Fred, brings up the importance of buffers.

There is agreement that all buffers should be monitored closely so there will be awareness, in advance, when resources along the critical path will be ready. Mark explains how important it is that people are warned when the time is approaching for them to drop anything else they are working on and work on the critical path. The students agree that a report monitoring all the buffers should be created and that highest priority should be given to any steps that reduce the project buffer. The report will be kept short, they decide, by not including steps that have already completed or are far off in the future.

Later, at the airport to meet his wife's incoming flight, Professor Rick runs into President vonBraun. As intimidating and presidential as ever, she asks him for an impromptu progress report. He indicates that impressive results are coming in from the different projects he's guiding at companies where his students work and he will be ready to approach them about sending more students to the Executive MBA program in a few months. She tells him he is wrong about the way he is going about it; that companies rarely send students; it's the prospective students themselves (mid level managers) who have to be persuaded.

COMMENTARY – CHAPTER 17

The importance of the contents of this chapter is often underestimated. So far, we have been dealing with the planning side of projects, but now we are introduced to the execution side. Project execution is THE most important part of achieving success using critical chain. In order to consistently shorten project times and meet delivery dates, behaviors must change. Monitoring and responding to the condition of the buffers is the key to that. Rather than responding to individual tasks, the project team responds to the condition of the buffers.

What is alluded to earlier in the book, but not covered in this chapter, are the measurements and policies that CAUSE the behaviors. Where is our poor shepherd without direction? He's simply wandering through the pastures, figuring it out by himself. Goldratt told us what the correct behaviors should be, but not how to create them. Let's look at a specific example. Remember that earlier we discussed the problem the project manager has focusing? Here is the solution to that problem.

Progress on the project is measured by the ratio of work to be completed to the amount of buffer remaining. The ratio tells us when a project is in danger of not being completed on time. For example, a project that has 100% of the work remaining and 100% of the buffer remaining has a ratio of 1:1; it's on schedule. A project that has 80% of the work remaining and 40% of the buffer remaining has a ratio of 8:4; clearly, it's at risk of not finishing on time. This is called the Buffer Burn Ratio. When tasks are delayed, they consume the buffer , potentially threatening the project completion date. By identifying which tasks are creating the highest buffer burn ratio, the project manager knows which task to focus on *right now*. His efforts can then be directed to solving that problem, thus causing the entire project to move forward.

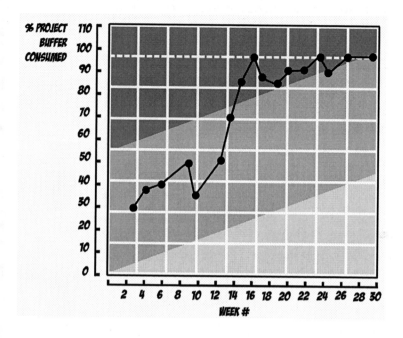

% PROJECT BUFFER CONSUMED

WEEK #

<u>Multiple Buffer Burn Ratio Calculations over Time</u>

Determination of the Buffer Burn Ratio isn't enough. It must be accompanied by management action. In order to create behavior, managers must respond to the measurement consistently. It's the management response that creates the actions within the organization and thereby overcomes the negative behaviors Goldratt outlined earlier: multi-tasking and the student syndrome. In this way, the response to the measurement causes behavior; buffer directed behavior.

Other measures of project progress must be brought into alignment with the Buffer Burn Ratio measurement. Stop focusing on

78

keeping everyone busy, releasing work into the system when it cannot be worked on anyway. The less excess work in the system, the less likely people are going to be distracted by doing the "wrong" work. Starting sooner doesn't mean finishing sooner, it means clogging the system with work that's not needed yet, confusing the organization's priorities, causing extra work to sort it out, and taking needed capacity away from the work at hand, causing more delays.

Stop measuring people on task completion dates. Instead, focus on rapid completion of the task at hand. If you really want people to give accurate estimates, you have to stop punishing them when the estimates they do provide turn out to be inaccurate. *Every* estimate you get will be "wrong." Get used to it. People should be working in a way very similar to relay racers: when they have the baton, they run as fast as possible. The rest of the time, they brace themselves, preparing to receive the baton.

During project execution, there are two things you should concern yourself with: 1. when there is a task for a resource to do, that he/she is working on it at full effort (without interruption) until completion and 2, you should be responding to situations where the Buffer Burn Ratio is showing that the project delivery date is at risk.

CHAPTER 18 – MANAGING SUBCONTRACTORS

Charlene, an accounting professor, asks Rick if she can sit in on his class. She is still trying to digest the "cost world" and the "throughput world" concepts they learned from Johnny.

Professor Rick begins his class by reiterating what they've learned from the Genemodem model. Then, he introduces another type of project — a project that, rather than being done by a company itself, is executed through the use of vendors and subcontractors. He points out that when choosing a vendor or subcontractor, price is a consideration, but so is lead-time. In fact, Rick says, a three-month delay could end up costing more (in lost revenue) than if they were to just give another 10% to all vendors across the board. Using one of his student's companies as an example, he draws his class through a calculation to quantify how much money will be lost in expected sales and drives the point home that most of it is unrecoverable. The company is investing six million to increase capacity and bring in an expected two million additional dollars in sales each month. The net margin on the company's product is more than 35 percent, so two million times 35 percent is seven hundred thousand, says Professor Rick. That is how much will be lost each month the plant expansion project is delayed. In some companies, there can also be a great deal of damage done to market share. It becomes clear just how important it is for all involved (every project leader as well as every project manager) to realize how big the penalties are for each month a project is delayed.

A student points out that everybody is conditioned to compete on price; that almost no one (companies and vendors alike) realizes that lead times are important — sometimes more important than price. Professor Rick advances the idea that if vendors are not asked to commit to a specified delivery date, money can be traded for shortened lead times. A student challenges Rick to talk to his vendor and make it happen. Rick agrees to a date on which he will do so.

At the vendor's, Rick, who does not yet understand how that particular business works, scans the proposal for clues, starts asking specific questions to nail down how long each part of the process takes. He comes up with a total of two weeks, not the six weeks the vendor alleges it will take. The vendor argues that the job cannot be assigned a top priority that will get it finished in two weeks. Rick asks him to make more profit on the job by trading lead-time for price. In the end, after the vendor has been assured he'll receive ample warning of when he can expect to receive the job, he agrees to deliver the critical part of the job in one week and the rest in four weeks — in exchange for more compensation than he originally requested.

COMMENTARY– CHAPTER 18

There's a problem with buffer directed behavior. It is one thing to direct your employees, but quite another to cause a vendor to change their behavior. How do you get an organization, over which you have limited control, to subordinate to your schedule? We want the same kind of behavior from our contractors that we expect from our own employees: we want them to work as quickly as they can without interruption.

So a new measure is introduced to contractors: delivery lead time; the time from placing the order to the time of delivery. You trade out the risk of late delivery for a price increase by offering an incentive to contractors for early delivery. As mentioned, one of the characters in this chapter proposes a 10% premium. Assuming the profit motive, most contractors will accept a higher than requested price in exchange for faster deliveries.

A second condition is laid out in order for this to work — advance booking of capacity. This requires a commitment on the project owner's part early in the project, even if it's a "handshake."

CHAPTER 19– MULTI-PROJECT ENVIRONMENTS

Back at Genemodem, the three members of the "think tank" talk with Isaac Levy, the executive VP of engineering who assigned them the project. So far, he is pleased with the outcome. The trio was charged with finding a way to significantly shrink development time and they found one, but by the time they implemented their changes, the A226 modem was already in the final stages.

Now, Levy wants to see how their method will work on a full project from start to finish.

Originally, the members of the think tank were promised ten thousand shares of Genemodem stock each if they succeeded. Now that they have, Levy asks them to gamble their newly ac-quired shares on a longer experiment to prove the viability of the method they developed. The trio agrees and asks for permission to hire more help from Rick Silver, their university professor who teaches them project management. They request and get a budget to pay him. Professor Rick and his wife, who have experienced many, many lean years in academia, are very pleased by this turn of events.

Rick starts his work for Genemodem and encounters a problem. He is not sure of how to proceed in a situation where multiple pro-jects share the same bottleneck. He takes his problem to Jim, his university department head, who has also been working hard to get up to speed with the ToC methodology. The first step is: IDEN-

TIFY the constraint. But, as they talk, Jim uses the word "bottle-neck" which he perceives as synonymous with "constraint." Rick points out that Jim is talking about production but in a project, the constraint is the critical path — so there is more than one constraint. Also, they are faced with multiple projects, each with its own critical path. If they try to deal with each project in isolation, they will be forced to ignore the bottleneck. They call on Johnny for help. Johnny remarks that he doesn't know enough about the project environment to be of help and Rick and Jim admit they don't know enough about constraints. The three agree to pool their knowledge in hopes of working out a solution.

COMMENTARY – CHAPTER 19

A common assumption in project management is that resources are infinite. The reason goes something like this: "The project deliverables are much more important than the cost of the resources. I can always get more when I need them." As a result, many projects are planned as though resources are unlimited. The problem is that of course, resources are neither unlimited nor immediately available when they're needed. This vital assumption is not verbalized, nor is it validated during the project planning process.

Goldratt is pointing out that often, resources can become bottlenecks in projects and consequently, they must be accounted for.

This is especially true when multiple projects share resources. When resources are shared among projects, the planning of any single project becomes much more difficult because it's hard to see how each individual resource will interact with the rest of the projects. In addition, the rate at which an organization can complete projects is regulated by the bottleneck resource. Goldratt is insinuating that there is more to the solution than he presents in **Critical Chain**. There is, in fact, quite a bit more to managing multiple projects beyond the basic elements offered so far.

IMPLICATIONS FOR MANAGEMENT

If bottleneck resources control the rate of project completions, then management must do two things:

1. Exploit this valuable resource to ensure it is not wasted.

2. Control the release of work to match the rate at which the bottleneck is working.

Controlling the release of work results in a "staggering" of projects to a "Drum" resource that controls the work rate for the entire system. By staggering the release, the priority system becomes much easier to manage. There is simply not as much work in the system at a time. This also eliminates the "wandering bottleneck" problem caused by fluctuating demand. Staggering projects level-loaded your system, smoothing the flow, reducing peak demands, accelerating the rate which *all* projects are completed..

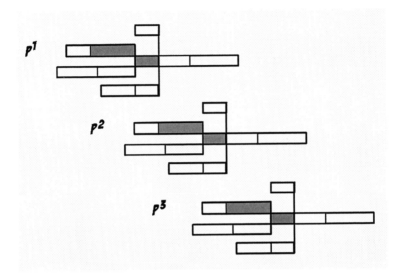

P¹

P²

P³

There is also the issue of implementation. Is it best to start your CCPM (Critical Chain Project Management) implementation with a fresh project or to start it with a project that's already in trouble? I've done it both ways. The problem with starting with a project that's already in progress is that there might not be enough time for the implemented changes to show improvement to the project. However, waiting until the next project start might delay the improvements to be gained. I prefer to start right away in order to get some results now rather than wait until the "ideal" conditions present themselves.

GLOSSARY – CHAPTER 19

Drum — The schedule for the bottleneck resource that dictates a pace of workflow for the entire organization. The term comes from the concept of a drummer in a band who sets the beat to which the entire band marches.

CHAPTER 20 – WHAT IF THE PROJECT IS COST PLUS?

Now Professor Rick is back in his own office and Ted, one of his students from the project management course comes in for help. Ted's having trouble calculating the damage that could be done by delaying the completion of a project. He can't find any damages; only advantages. He explains that he works for a subcontractor and at the time a contract is signed, pricing is low because very aggressive price cutting has taken place to get the contract. The real profit will come later, when changes are made in the project, generating more profit. The subcontractor will make as many changes as desired/needed — very happily. The longer the project duration and the more changes there are, the more money they will make. They have no incentive to finish sooner because they get progress payments all along the way. So, Ted says, as the subcontractor, delays don't bother his company; only the company that hired them has an incentive to finish early.

Rick explains that over the long run the construction subcontractor can, indeed, be negatively impacted when the ability for the developer to profit from a finished project and recover initial investment is postponed. If the development company is hurt — maybe even bankrupted — by delays, when it comes time to look for the next contract, the subcontractor may discover that the developer is no longer in business. Clearly, prolonging the project and "milking" it for change fees is short sighted. The best incentive to reduce completion times is a healthy customer and more business in the future.

After Ted leaves, Johnny stops by. Professor Rick shares his theory about augmenting vendor payments as a way to get improved delivery performance. Johnny points out that Rick's idea creates a win-lose situation by making the company pay extra for something that should be inherent in the price. According to the Theory of Constraints, win-lose situations do not exist and if it seems as though they do, the problem is being looked at too narrowly. Johnny suggests an alternative: because the construction industry is price-driven, he proposes a system that uses hefty bonuses for beating the promise date and similarly weighted penalties for missing it. The developer will get a much higher return on his investment by being able to offer the developed properties for sale sooner and thereby be able to pay off his loans sooner while the "fast" subcontractor will be amply rewarded.

COMMENTARY – CHAPTER 20

For some projects, there is little immediate financial incentive to finish early. Even in these situations, Goldratt makes the argument that it's best for the long-term to focus on reducing the project lead time; perhaps your customer won't be around tomorrow. That's not a very satisfying or realistic reason to change the culture of the project management organization. For example, a defense contractor selling to governments is just one of many situations in which we doubt that the customer is going away.

A more compelling reason for reducing project lead time is the impact it has on your attractiveness to the market. Companies with reliable deliveries and short response are at a premium — if you can deliver reliably, you can hold on to the customers you have and attract more new ones. You will, despite a higher price, be more attractive to customers, ensuring an enduring place in the market. If your organization relies on projects, you should be *expert* in this mission-critical process.

Goldratt, though indirectly, is pointing out the "Spirit of ToC" in solving problems. The spirit of ToC says that you should strive for win/win solutions in all of your dealings. If you're the prime contractor, and you have suppliers that behave as if the project can go on forever, you have to find a way to motivate them. A way to create the right behavior is to offer significant bonuses for early completion and impose penalties for late finishes. The prime contractor is rewarded by early achievement of the benefits of the project, and so is the company that gave them the contract. This alignment (win/win) is fundamental to creating sustained progress.

CHAPTER 21 – A SOLUTION TO DECLINING ENROLLMENTS

Professor Rick receives a message to call Mr. Brad Newbolt. The name is new to him. Newbolt turns out to be the president of Q.E.C., a company where one of Rick's students works and where they have implemented some of the methods he is teaching. Newbolt asks Rick to speak to an organization of company presidents at their upcoming dinner meeting. The professor sends his own president a memo telling her that he has been invited to speak. When he arrives at the meeting, she is the very first person he sees. VonBraun tells him that she had to pull strings in order to be there. Rick gives his talk and feels he has done well. Then, those company presidents who have already tried Rick's methods begin to share their experiences, all of which are quite positive. VonBraun remarks about how much money the methods must be worth to the companies and presses them to send more students to the university's Executive MBA program. They commit to sending more if they can be assured that the students will learn more about what they heard during Rick's dinner talk. Once outside, vonBraun asks Rick if he thinks it's possible to create a full, two-year program that will bring real value to the students. He definitely thinks it's possible and he is no longer worried about tenure.

COMMENTARY - CHAPTER 21

This chapter indicates the cause of the declining enrollments in the MBA programs is a lack of courses that offer workable methods and know-how. Theoretically, as classes incorporate the study of more useful techniques, companies will send more workers to attend university MBA programs. We're not sure if the cause identified in **Critical Chain** exists in reality, but it seems plausible that if the universities teach information that is practical, they can attract more students. It also seems right because so many educational firms that specialize in offering real-world know-how exist today, and they are not suffering from a lack of students.

CHAPTER 22 — DEFINING THE CRITICAL CHAIN

Now Professor Rick is back in his classroom looking over his original outline for the course, trying to see which topic he hasn't yet covered in as much depth as he could or should have. He considers reiterating the conceptual difference between a project buffer, feeding buffer, and a resource buffer and wonders how many of his students understand that resource buffers don't change the elapsed time of the project. Good subject, he thinks. He goes with it. But, one of his students interrupts with a real-world problem.

It's Ruth, part of the Genemodem trio, and she is worried that if her company is late on one of the non-critical paths and the entire feeding buffer is already exhausted, they might start to consume the project buffer. Fred, another member of think tank from Genemodem wonders if it's true that the critical path has changed and now begins where the problem is located. He goes on to explain that they only put feeding buffers where a non-critical path merges into the critical path — so a change in the critical path will make it necessary to change the locations of many of the feeding buffers. Now Mark, the third member of the trio, reiterates that the critical path has been defined as the longest (in time) chain of dependent events.

The class knows that changing the location of the feeding buffers every time a delay develops on a non-critical path isn't a workable solution, but they recognize the need to protect this newly emerged critical path from disruptions. So, they must move the critical path, yet they can't.

Trying to find the erroneous assumption, Professor Rick writes a cloud. He notes that the objective is to finish the project on time. Next, he determines the two opposing but necessary conditions: they cannot afford to rearrange everything, yet they cannot leave the true critical path exposed, so they can't formally change the critical path. Rick decides that rearranging the project midway; formally changing the critical path is the least desirable of the two conditions. He asks the class what assumption is made when they say that the critical path will be exposed if it is not formally changed, and if the true critical path is really very different from the new critical path. It is determined that the two paths are actually the same after they merge, so the only place where any real exposure exists is up to and just short of the step where they merge.

Now another student speaks up and says he is having the same problem, only worse. The student draws his situation on the board. It appears that one resource (a specialist) is overloaded and as the specialist switches from one non-critical path to another, the delays do, too. And so, it becomes clear that dependent steps ("dependencies") that can be performed by the same resource (that has limited capacity) must be performed sequentially rather than in parallel.

Dependencies, Professor Rick concludes, can result from a path or common resource. In general, the longest chain will be composed of sections that are path dependent and sections that are resource dependent.

So, short of altering the definition of critical path, it is apparent that an additional name is needed for the "other" chain of steps they have identified as constituting the constraint, but that nobody is any longer calling "critical path." They name the longest chain of dependent steps the "critical chain" and summarize that as long as resource contentions are present, the critical chain might be very different than the critical path.

From there, Professor Rick and his students move into a discussion of how to sequence the steps that comprise the chain. They conclude the sequence doesn't matter because the project buffer will diminish the effects of any uncertainties that are present. Rick concedes that there are, however, specific projects where the contentions are too big for the feeding buffers.

COMMENTARY – CHAPTER 22

There are two issues tackled here:

1. "Shifting" of the critical path during execution
2. Dealing with resource contention

WHEN THE FEEDING BUFFERS ARE EXHAUSTED

What happens when the buffer on the feeding path is eliminated? Should the critical path be redefined? How stable is the critical path? If the feeding path is delayed to the point where it consumes the feeding buffer, then the longest path is no longer the critical path, it's a "new" critical path. So as a project manager, you have to decide whether or not to re-plan the project. The logical response would be to change the project plan. However, changing the critical path only changes it up to the point where the two paths, the critical path and the non-critical path merge. Afterwards, the path is the same. Since the critical path changes very little, changing the critical path has no advantage. If you focus on the longest path all the time, whether or not you call it the "critical" path has little meaning, since you are always focusing on the longest chain of tasks — the very definition of the critical path.

DEALING WITH RESOURCE CONTENTION

Experienced project managers realize that when resource contention is encountered, tasks are delayed. Resource dependency has as much of an impact on project completion as task dependency. Thus, to effectively plan and execute the project, resource contention must be identified and resolved. This resolution of contention, task sequencing, results in the critical chain. The critical chain is the longest sequence of dependent tasks including resource dependency.

96

What effect does the addition of buffers have on the project? Do buffers expand or reduce the time the project takes to complete? Goldratt makes a statement that adding buffers does not increase project lead time at all, although he does not substantiate it in the text. The case for his assertion lies in the statistical reality of the central limit theorem. When tasks with 50% probability are added together, the sum of the tasks with no safety is shorter than when tasks with safety are added together. So, the path is actually shorter when adding tasks of 50% probability together with a buffer to compensate for variability of the path as a whole.

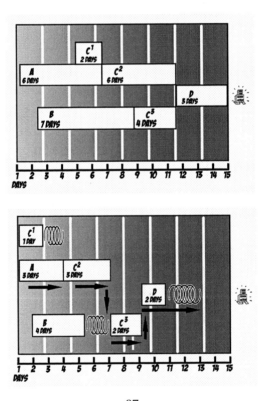

GLOSSARY - CHAPTER 22

Critical Chain —The longest chain of activity and resource dependencies considering both technological (task) precedence and resource contention. The constraint of a project. The critical chain plus the project buffer defines the lead time for the project.

CHAPTER 23 – TOC OFFERS REAL SOLUTIONS TO BUSINESS PROBLEMS

VonBraun wants to attract more students to the Executive MBA program, so she wants the program to answer real and current needs. Companies want program graduates who bring them value. Vowing to thoroughly indoctrinate students in the "throughput world," vonBraun launches a special program centered on ToC.

COMMENTARY – CHAPTER 23

Universities *should* be teaching ToC to MBA students so they can acquire practical information that will be useful in real world applications.

CHAPTER 24 – WHAT IF THE BOTTLENECK MOVES?

Mark, one of Professor Rick's students from Genemodem, clarifies that while critical chain eliminates resource contention from within a single project, it does nothing about the resource contention that can exist between projects in a multi-project environment. Another student, Ted, interjects with a definition the professor feels the class already understands. He recaps the meaning of resource contention as a situation in which the same resource is supposed to do two different steps at once. The problem, he continues, is deciding which step to postpone. Each project leader will fight not to have his step postponed, Ted says. Mark remarks that even one deviation in timing can tighten scheduling to the point where contentions will multiply.

Professor Rick wants to know what the conceptual mistake is. He asks why they are considering contentions as significant when contentions only account for a small amount of time compared to the project path as a whole. Rick continues, questioning whether the buffers would absorb the contentions if they were just left alone. He asks his students if they've seen similar problems elsewhere and it turns out that they have. A student explains that it crops up in production when work piles up in front of a machine and it isn't plain which job is to be processed first.

It becomes clear that the answer of what to do in a projects situation is to follow the example of how the same problem is dealt with in production: IDENTIFY the bottleneck and then EXPLOIT it (schedule the work sequence for the bottleneck), then SUBORDINATE all other resources. The result also becomes clear: most of the overloads from the other resources will be removed and the buffer will absorb any sporadic peaks of load that still exist.

Rick draws out from his students that a bottleneck in a production environment will create havoc when attempting to synchronize between projects and that, just as it does in production, the same impact can occur in projects. Moreover, not protecting the bottleneck from Murphy by using buffers results in wasting time on the bottleneck — which, consequently, results in a reduction in the overall throughput of the organization. Fewer projects are delivered than could have been.

The class sums up and brings the discussion to a conclusion. It must be remembered that to protect the bottleneck, another buffer must be inserted: the bottleneck buffer. The feeding buffers provide early warning and if a resource contention starts to exhaust one feeding buffer after another, it's time to declare it a resource constraint.

COMMENTARY— CHAPTER 24

Since the rate at which projects can be accomplished is dictated by the bottleneck resource, any work stoppages reduce the number of projects that can be done. Therefore, the organization should take steps to make certain the bottleneck is protected from such disruptions by adding another buffer, the bottleneck buffer. This buffer ensures there is always an available supply of work for the bottleneck so project throughput can remain uninterrupted.

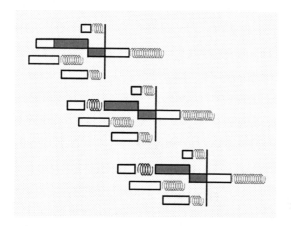

GLOSSARY — CHAPTER 24

Bottleneck Buffer — The bottleneck constraint buffer is a multi-project tool used to offset the work on the most heavily loaded resource to minimize queuing.

Syn: Capacity Constraint Buffer (Leach), Strategic Resource Buffer (Newbold,).

CHAPTER 25 – HOW TO MANAGE A PORTFOLIO OF PROJECTS

In this final chapter, UniCo asks the university to develop new know-how. Top managers need help with the decision process and what the university has offered so far is geared only to work levels that go from project leaders down.

UniCo's Don Pederson is working on the new facility his company is building. He knows additional investments are going to be requested and asks for advice on investment justification.

This prompts Charlene, the accounting professor at the university, to talk about "dollar days" (a measure of the amount of time money is invested without return) and how this approach provides a much more accurate way to evaluate investment alternatives. She notes that physicists know that one of the most important rules is conservation of momentum, where the summation of the masses of all the parts in a system multiplied by their corresponding velocity is conserved, no matter what happens inside the system. Charlene makes a direct comparison to a method of making investments in tiny steps. Suppose, she begins, that you invest two dollars. After one day, you are invested for two "dollar days." After five days, you are invested for ten "dollars days." Then, at that point, you get back (flush out) your original investment. You are still in the hole for the number of "dollar days," Charlene points out, because your investment was tied up and unavailable to you. The point is thereby made that while we regard money and investment as almost synonymous, they are vastly different. While money is measured in dollars, investment is measured in "dollar days."

COMMENTARY – CHAPTER 25

The concept of "flush" is explained quite nicely here. Essentially, the return on investment does not begin until you have your cash back; compensating for the time it was tied up. Goldratt is also pointing us to the fact that critical chain is more than just a device for planning and execution, it's a tool to help managers to make better decisions about which projects to work on — a tool to manage a portfolio of projects.

And the book ends.

GLOSSARY – CHAPTER 25

Dollar Days — The total number of days your investment was tied up and unavailable to you in terms of return on your money. Expressed as a ratio of dollars: days

Flush — A decision making tool that measures the value of cash-time from investment to recovery.

APPENDIX

ALL PROJECTS HAVE PROBLEMS

The two major problems with ALL projects are that they are late and cost too much. There is empirical evidence to back this claim. The Standish Group studied IT projects in the late 90s and found the following:

∞ 30% of projects are cancelled before they finished — they simply run out of steam.

∞ 75% of completed projects are late and don't finish by the original projected date.

∞ Average cost overruns are 189%.

∞ Average time overruns are 222%.

Of course, the problem is not limited to IT projects. As Goldratt points out in **Critical Chain**, there are numerous examples of projects that finish late and cost too much. The common response to late delivery is to reduce scope, take features out until the next release of the product, identify some aspects are "not that important," or sacrifice reliability. These are the types of compromises to which he is referring.

These are not the only problems in projects, however. Typically we find too many changes, excessive rework, priority battles, and resource constraints. So, how do we solve them? Typical solutions to problems found in projects are:

- ∞ **Require more detailed planning** — if we can get to the "right" level of detail ahead of time, there will be fewer surprises at the end. The assumption behind this solution is that we can control the uncertainty, or at least most of it. It's all about having a good plan.

- ∞ **Assign more project managers to smaller bits of the project.** If the sheep are getting lost, we must need more shepherds, right? The assumption is that project management is essentially a span-of-control problem.

- ∞ **Reclaim delegated authority that has been pushed down to lower levels in the organization.** The assumption here is similar to that in the problem above, except we need better shepherds.

- ∞ **Move accountability further down the organization.** It's the opposite of the above and the same assumption as with span-of-control. Let's have a job fair and recruit more shepherds!

- ∞ **Re-plan the project more frequently.** We know we can't see very far into the future. So, as we get into the project, we'll learn more and make a better plan. Instead of revisiting the plan every quarter, we'll do it every month. We'll require the shepherds to report in more frequently, and they must bring their sheep so management can count them.

∞ **Implement sophisticated planning models** — we should buy software for the shepherds to manage their sheep more effectively. The husbandry module has a browser interface and you can forecast the precise percentage of sheep that will mate and produce more sheep. We can input forecasted weather patterns and other significant factors and come up with a probability factor for producing a full herd next spring. Again, the assumption is that the problem with project performance is poor planning (which, of all the possibilities, is probably closest to the truth).

∞ Longer, more intense prayers on the part of project managers! Only God can save us on this project!

THE THEORY OF CONSTRAINTS

ToC is a set of holistic processes and insights, all based on a systems approach that simplifies the improving and managing of complex organizations by focusing on the few physical and logical constraining "leverage" points. Furthermore, it provides a tool set to build and implement the "levers" (holistic rules) that will synchronize the parts to achieve an order of magnitude improvement in the performance of the system as a whole.

ToC is not just a tool to manage bottlenecks. In fact, the scope of tools and breadth of application of ToC is substantial. In the graphic, you can see that critical chain project management is just a subset, *one* of the generic solutions of ToC.

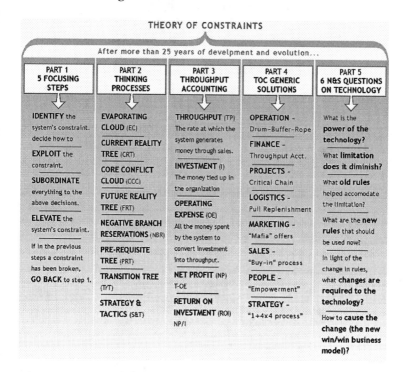

THEORY OF CONSTRAINTS

After more than 25 years of develpment and evolution...

PART 1 5 FOCUSING STEPS	PART 2 THINKING PROCESSES	PART 3 THROUGHPUT ACCOUNTING	PART 4 TOC GENERIC SOLUTIONS	PART 5 6 N&S QUESTIONS ON TECHNOLOGY
IDENTIFY the system's constraint. decide how to	**EVAPORATING CLOUD** (EC)	**THROUGHPUT** (TP) The rate at which the system generates money through sales.	**OPERATION -** Drum–Buffer–Rope	What is the **power of the technology?**
EXPLOIT the constraint.	**CURRENT REALITY TREE** (CRT)		**FINANCE -** Throughput Acct.	What **limitation does it diminish?**
SUBORDINATE everything to the above decisions.	**CORE CONFLICT CLOUD** (CCC)	**INVESTMENT** (I) The money tied up in the organization	**PROJECTS -** Critical Chain	What **old rules** helped accomodate the limitation?
ELEVATE the system's constraint.	**FUTURE REALITY TREE** (FRT)	**OPERATING EXPENSE** (OE)	**LOGISTICS -** Pull Replenishment	What are the **new rules** that should
If in the previous steps a constraint has been broken, **GO BACK** to step 1.	**NEGATIVE BRANCH RESERVATIONS** (NBR)	All the money spent by the system to convert investment into throughput.	**MARKETING -** "Mafia" offers	be used now?
	PRE-REQUISITE TREE (PRT)		**SALES -** "Buy-in" process	In light of the change in rules,
	TRANSITION TREE (TrT)	**NET PROFIT** (NP) T-OE	**PEOPLE -** "Empowerment"	what **changes are required to the technology?**
	STRATEGY & TACTICS (S&T)	**RETURN ON INVESTMENT** (ROI) NP/I	**STRATEGY -** "1+4x4 process"	How to **cause the change (the new win/win business model)?**

CASCADE EFFECT

Late completions cascade through the project and across projects. This is called the "Cascade Effect". Essentially, the cascade effect refers to late task finishes causing delays throughout the project and early finishes never being recognized. It's fundamental to the nature of projects and the core reason why they are often late.

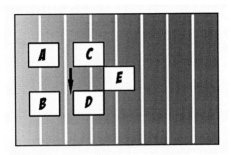

In the diagram above, you see that if task A is late, it does not matter how early task B completes, task D will be delayed, and thus the project. Conversely, if A finishes early, it still doesn't help, because D must wait for B to complete.

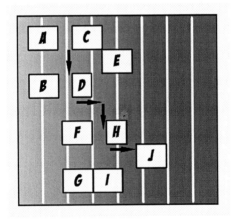

When the same resource works on multiple projects, we see the same effect, except that both projects are now delayed because of a single task. This is the essence of the cascade effect. Delays multiply, but gains do not add up.

CRITICAL CHAIN RESULTS

Organization	Before	After
Next Generation Wireless Technology Product Development Airgo Networks	Cycle time from first silicon to production for 1st generation was 19 months.	Cycle time from first silicon to production for 2nd generation was 8 months.
Automotive Product Development DaimlerChrysler	Cycle time for prototype builds was 10 weeks.	Cycle time for prototype builds is 8 weeks. Delivery date performance increased by 83 % with much less fire fighting.
Telecommunications Network Design and Installation eircom, Ireland	On-time delivery less than 75%. Average cycle time was 70 days.	Increased on-time delivery to 98+ %. Average cycle time dropped to 30 days.
Biotechnology Plant Engineering Genencor	20% projects on time.	87% projects slated to complete on time, with approximately 15% immediate increase in throughput
Home Appliances New Product Development Hamilton Beach/ Proctor-Silex	34 new products per year. 74% projects on time.	Increased throughput to 52 new products in 1st year, and to 70+ in 2nd year, with no increase in headcount. 88% projects on time.
High Tech New Product Development HP Digital Camera Group	6 cameras launched in 2004. 1 camera launched in spring window. 1 out of 6 cameras launched on time.	15 cameras launched in 2005, with 25% lower R&D expenses. 7 cameras launched in spring window. All 15 cameras launched on time.
ASIC Design Technology Development LSI Logic	74% projects on time for small projects; major tool releases were late.	Due-date performance increased to 85% projects on time; major tools released on time for three years in a row.
Telecomm Switches Design, Development and Upgrades Lucent Technologies		300 to 400 active projects with 30 + deliveries a month. Cycle times are 10 to 25% shorter while throughput per person higher by 45%.

Organization	Before	After
High Tech Medical Product Development Medtronic	1 software release every 6-9 months. Predictability was poor on device programs.	1 software release every two months. Substantial improvement in delivering device programs on time.
Electrical Power Transmission, Engineer-to-Order ABB AG, Power Technologies Division	Throughput was 300 bays per year.	Throughput increased to 430 bays per year.
Food Preparation and Packaging Oregon Freeze Dry	72 sales projects completed per year.	171 sales projects completed per year. 52% increase in throughput dollars.
Garment Design Skye Group	Product ranges were late to market.	100% due-date performance. 30% reduction in lead times and sampling costs.
Warfighter Systems Testing US Air Force Operational Test & Evaluation Center	18 projects in six months. On time delivery unknown.	26 projects in six months. 75% projects on time; 30% reduction in cycle time.
Aircraft Repair & Overhaul US Air Force, Warner Robins Air Logistics Center, C5 Production Line	Turn around time (TAT) 240 days. 13 aircrafts in repair cycle.	Turn around time (TAT) 160 days. 7 aircrafts in repair cycle.
Aircraft Repair & Overhaul US Marine Corps Logistics Base, Barstow, CA	Repair cycle time (RCT) for MK48 was 168 days. RCT for LAV25 was 180 days. RCT for MK14 was 152 days. RCT for LAVAT was 182 days.	Repair cycle time (RCT) for MK48 is 82 days. RCT for LAV25 is 124 days. RCT for MK14 is 59 days. RCT for LAVAT is 122 days.
Aircraft Repair and Overhaul US Naval Aviation Depot, Cherry Point	Average turnaround time (TAT) for H-46 aircrafts was 225 days. Average turnaround time (TAT) for H-53 aircrafts was 310 days; throughput was 23 per year.	Reduced TAT to 167 days, a 25% reduction while work scope was increasing. Reduced TAT to 180 days, a 41% reduction; delivered 23 aircrafts in six months (throughput of 46 per year). 70% reduction in backshop backlog due to better synchronization on aircraft lines.

Organization	Before	After
Submarine Maintenance and Repair US Naval Shipyard, Pearl Harbor	Job Completion Rate = 94%. On-time delivery less than 60%. Cost per job was $5,043.	Job Completion Rate increased to 98%. Increased on-time delivery to 95+%. Reduced cost per job to $3,355, a 33% reduction; manning dropped by 25%. Overtime reduced by 49%, a $9M saving in first year.

Reported by Realization Technologies, Inc. Website
Reprinted with permission ©2005

IMPLEMENTING CRITICAL CHAIN

Critical Chain Practitioners at both the 2004 and 2005 Project Flow conferences have shown that significant gains are possible with Critical Chain. They also stressed that implementation must be swift. Once you decide to implement Critical Chain, it is important to forge the new system while the iron is hot. If you don't start getting results in two to three months, the implementation will become difficult.

Below are the key lessons in implementing Critical Chain.

LESSON: IMPLEMENT THE THREE RULES, NO MORE NO LESS!

All the implementation challenges fall under either achieving buy-in or establishing robust mechanics. It is very easy to spend a lot of energy in those areas by educating everyone thoroughly, tweaking data endlessly, customizing reports etc.

To not get overwhelmed, we must remind ourselves that Critical Chain is about implementing its three rules:

1. **Pipelining**: Stagger project starts

2. **Buffering**: Shorten cycle times, include 50% buffers

3. **Buffer Management**: Follow task priorities, don't waste buffers

It is impossible to implement these rules piecemeal. All three have to be implemented from the get-go, without compromise. Any concession will only show up as resistance to change or cumbersome mechanics. For example:

∞ Organizations doing large projects tend to implement Critical Chain one project at a time. They compromise the PIPELIN-ING rule. When projects are not staggered, resource conflicts are bound to arise. Buffers get consumed and commitments are missed. Project Managers do not cut cycle times. Task Managers cannot follow task priorities. Very quickly, faith in the new system is lost.

∞ Many times organizations initially aim to just deliver projects on time without increasing speed and throughput. They com-promise the BUFFERING rule (cycle times are not cut, but buffers are added). When cycle times are not cut, PIPELIN-ING rule also has to be compromised because staggering the projects would cause all due-dates to be pushed far out. When projects are not pipelined, BUFFER MANAGEMENT cannot be done. The entire system falls apart.

∞ Some managers compromise the BUFFER MANAGEMENT rule because they feel it is "micromanagement". In reality, without management, buffers get wasted which creates a feel-ing that shorter cycle times are unrealistic. Sooner or later the organization reverts to its old ways (not staggering project starts; hiding safeties in project plans, and setting priorities ad hoc in execution). Instead of reacting to symptoms when we hit roadblocks, it is better to diagnose which of the rules has been compromised.

LESSON: IMPLEMENT IN EIGHT SIMPLE STEPS

The following eight simple steps keep everyone focused on the three rules, while achieving buy-in's and establishing robust mechanics:

1. **Create management consensus on business needs:** Do not pursue Critical Chain for the sake of adopting a "best practice". Use business needs to drive the implementation.

1. **Get buy-in on improvement potential:** Managers have to be convinced about the waste before they will adopt new rules. A useful technique is to enumerate and quantify the losses from Interruptions and Parkinson's Law.

2. **Get buy-in on the 3 rules and set ambitious targets:**

3. To ensure that managers are not just paying lip service to the three rules but are committed, *they* should be asked to set ambitious improvement targets.

4. **Design the solution:** Mechanics cannot be perfect in the beginning, but a few items must be figured out up-front: roles of master scheduler, project managers and task man-

114

agers; project architecture; and policy-type changes. Everything else can be adjusted later on.

5. **Create pipeline plan and validate it:** Check that the overall pipeline plan meets throughput targets. If it does not, re-evaluate the targets or cut cycle times across-the-board.

6. **Establish Task Management:** Task Management is the cornerstone of Buffer Management in multi-project environments. Task Management is monitoring remaining duration; and allowing tasks to be executed with minimal interruptions and in the right order of priority.

7. **Establish surrounding processes**: Put in place the pipeline, project and resource management processes.

8. *Use Buffer Diagnostics (and ToC's 5 Focusing Steps) to continue improving:* Only ongoing improvement can guarantee a sustained implementation. Use Buffer Diagnostics to guide local improvements, and the Five Focusing Steps to guide business-level improvements.

LESSON: TOP MANAGEMENT MUST PLAY AN ACTIVE ROLE

Sponsorship is not enough. Even though the top managers' role is to set policies and make planning-time decisions (execution is delegated to middle mangers and frontline managers), in successful implementations the top managers play a more active role for the first 6 to 12 months by:

- **Setting Aggressive Goals:** Only when aggressive goals are set that substantial improvements happen. An organization is more easily galvanized around ambitious goals than incremental improvements. For example, though people were overloaded and projects running behind, HP Digital Camera group set an audacious target of going from 6 new cameras in a year to 15. They actually achieved their target, delivering all projects on time with an implementation that went live in six weeks.

- **Creating a Habit of Managing Buffers:** Close oversight by top management is necessary until Buffer Management becomes second nature. For example, the senior leadership in Warner Robins ALC go on daily rounds and personally get involved in resolving issues.

- **Not Delegating the Implementation Until Transition is Complete:** Only top management can proactively identify and eliminate policy obstacles. For example, John Quigley, VP of Engineering at the rapidly growing Airgo Networks, stays involved in pipelining, task management and even training new managers. By implementing the three rules in eight simple steps, with top management playing an active role, it is possible to achieve success swiftly and surely.

Reported by Realization Technologies, Inc. © 2005 (reprinted with permission)

IMPLEMENTATION CASE STUDY

<u>Pit Crews cut assembly time in half, giving
FMC Energy Systems "The Racer's Edge."</u>

By Thayer Bennett

Forget the greasy stereotype and think about the neat, sharply
synchronized pit crews of today. They represent optimum speed,
precise timing and meticulous attention to detail. Those same
benefits can be driven right onto the factory floor, giving the
manufacturer a competitive workflow advantage that's hard to beat.
As part of their "Plan for Manufacturing Excellence," Pinnacle
Strategies harnessed a pit crew analogy (The Pinnacle Pit Crew
Method[SM]) to demonstrate and facilitate successful Critical Chain
Project Management (CCPM). The innovative idea proved itself by
turning in an outstanding performance in a recent application at
FMC Energy Systems, an engineer-to-order manufacturer of com-
plex capital equipment in Houston.

When demand outpaced capacity at FMC Energy Systems, it was
imperative to ramp up production. The company hired the Pinnacle team to identify areas where immediate improvement was possible, then formulate and initiate solutions. Pinnacle complied,
coupling considerable experience implementing Critical Chain projects with their "pit crew" technique and other innovative strategies. The outcome was impressive. Pinnacle CEO Mark Woeppel
reports that the project resulted in a 50% reduction in test duration

and final assembly time for the products FMC Energy Systems made for Shell Oil and substantial improvement overall including an increase in labor productivity of 15 to 30 percent — all without capital investment — and within 60 days.

Driller demand for FMC Energy Systems' subsea trees (the huge under-ocean structures that interface between wellheads and flow lines) increased dramatically as the call for oil grew worldwide and surged in the U.S. Of all of the means utilized by the company to increase speed to market (physical expansion of the plant, increased standardization, quality initiatives, etc.), Pinnacle's Critical Chain implementation that incorporated the development of pit crews for the manufacturing operation proved to be "most significant," according to Kendall Turner, FMC Energy Systems Assembly Process Engineering Manager. By relating the tree assembly process to a racecar making a pit stop, the method of working was changed so that workers were "at the ready" with the right parts at the right time. Relating the process to a pit stop also provided a rationale for talking in already-familiar terms and consequently, downtime associated with the learning curve that might have come from introducing a "Critical Chain" vocabulary was completely avoided. The end result of using these methods was that problems were acted on immediately and the time it took to build the final product was cut in half. The shift in methodology was one of moving from problem solving after the fact to clearly defined anticipation and the proactive execution of needed procedures.

Subsea trees are very large (three or more stories tall in the case of some vertical tree structures) and extremely complex, made up of literally thousands of parts. There is a need to create many redundant systems and in order to meet emerging customer needs engineering is necessarily ongoing during production. The manufacture of these multi-million dollar pieces of equipment is a daunting task requiring superb process coordination and control. When Pinnacle entered the scene, the existing FMC Energy Systems situation was one of such record sales demands that assembly was pushed to the limits. Lead times were too long, completion times were too variable and defect rates were unacceptable. "Based on initial analysis," said Pinnacle Project Manager and Senior Consultant Bruce Nelson, "our immediate objective was to increase the production rate by reducing assembly time." The large majority of the time the product was in production, it sat idle waiting to be worked on or waiting for decisions to be made. Assemblers were often out of the area chasing down parts, tools, fixtures, materials handling equipment and approvals and consequently, they were functioning like drivers without a car. A change in emphasis from keeping people moving to keeping the product moving was necessary. Pinnacle recommended that careful identification and pre-staging of parts and equipment needed for each "lap" in FMC Energy Systems' subsea tree assembly "race" would eliminate a great deal of down time. A comparison to a racecar making a pit stop helped workers see that time previously wasted in assembly slowdowns and stoppages, thought to be inherent in the process, could be recovered.

"Pinnacle's Scott Button," said Nelson, "helped create a breakdown structure, sequencing all of the assembly tasks in proper order and setting up a load path. Once FMC Energy Systems workers could see what was coming up three to five days in advance, they were able to make all the preparations that were needed before the part actually entered their segment of the assembly process." Nelson continued, "We equated it to knowing which lap a car is going to come into the pit and working ahead to put new tires on rims and make sure they're inflated to the proper pressure in order to insure quick action to get the car moving again — action that could begin the second the car stopped. Simple as it sounds, changing the way the workers viewed their process had a huge impact. Without the need to hire more workers or invest in more equipment, FMC Energy Systems' production capacity doubled."

Pinnacle's plan to reduce assembly lead-time while maintaining or improving product quality was comprehensive. The strategy was to create activity that was "event" rather than "date" driven. In the process of analyzing the work and executing the strategy, they utilized parallel work paths, measured daily progress, demanded accountability, and left no detail to chance. A network of specific tasks was created, optimum task sequence was determined, time durations were plotted, resource requirements were identified and a workable schedule was shaped.

Early in their implementation, the Pinnacle Strategies team conducted exhaustive on-site analysis to determine the locations of bottleneck and/or constraint operations within the assembly area. A race leader was appointed and the pit crew was assigned the task of isolating and understanding any current issue stopping or hampering assembly. The crew was also charged with providing, with the help of management-mandated support from Production Control, Engineering, Quality Control or Purchasing, on-the-spot remedies to quickly get the assembly process moving again. In order to function at optimal level, the initial pit crew was made up of seasoned personnel chosen, not just based on experience, but on the possession of a "pioneering" mindset.

Accountabilities were changed to give the race leader primary responsibility for on-time delivery, product lead-time and organizational responsibility for the assembly pit crew. The pit crew had responsibility for both "proactive" and "reactive" functions. The proactive duties included planning and organization of scheduled work tasks, making sure tools, equipment, service providers and procedures had been reviewed and tested and were ready for use. Reactive functions involved problem solving using techniques such as root cause analysis to get to the bottom of recurring dilemmas. Creation of the race team with its pit crew also served to temper the inevitable culture shock that comes when workers are required to change from working from a list of functions to working within a closely guided plan. No longer something to react to, problems were now being anticipated (three to five tasks ahead) and the future was becoming predictable and manageable.

Once the FMC Energy Systems "race team" was in place it was time to roll out the rest of the Pinnacle implementation strategy. New scheduling processes were unveiled, then a measurement system. Organizational behaviors that could be used to support a more seamlessly continuous assembly of trees were identified. Improvements to the process were put into action and then reviewed in terms of impact on reduction of overall lead times. Management skills were honed. Finally, an additional team to "cross pollinate" advantages to other assembly areas within the Houston plant was developed. All along the way, the implementation was solidly structured down to the detail level, such as in providing for the handling of problems that could not be resolved by the pit crew.

FUNDAMENTAL CHANGES WITH HUGE IMPACT

Pinnacle Strategies identified the most significant and pivotal opportunities to improve assembly methods and practices at FMC Energy Systems. How even a single change can reap impressive results is exemplified by the efficiency gained when the manufacturing line was reconfigured. Pinnacle recommended that, rather than using all available bays to build trees, a quarter of them be reallocated to allow for the building of tubing hangers in parallel. The resulting gain in speed provided a solid benchmark in performance improvement.

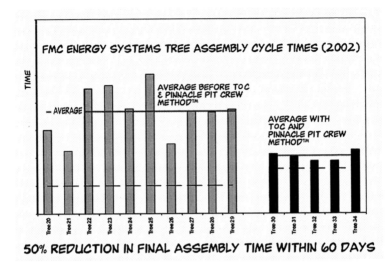

50% REDUCTION IN FINAL ASSEMBLY TIME WITHIN 60 DAYS

Another particularly important stride was taken when Pinnacle introduced the posting of "critical measures" on the FMC Energy Systems shop floor by using a "dashboard" that gave everyone an at-a-glance picture of performance, such as the tracking of the amount of buffering built into a schedule. Because workers in different categories needed different reports and statistics, information was provided on a variety of levels. Posted measurements included the schedule status of what jobs were on time, behind or ahead and they were refreshed daily as data was collected from the pit crew leader and others. Lead-time performance was also posted. The information made it easy to enforce accountability, which, in turn, proved invaluable in bringing previously hidden obstacles into view so they could be resolved.

"To sum it up," explained Pinnacle CEO Mark Woeppel, "implementing improvement successfully isn't about changing everything, it's about knowing how to apply the right change in the right way, but the most important ingredient of all is working with a great company that's committed to supporting a carefully conceived and executed plan for manufacturing excellence. FMC Energy Systems is just that kind of company."

Presenting the FMC Energy Systems perspective, Robert (Bob) Houlgrave, the company's Shell Alliance Manager stated, "Mark Woeppel's group [Pinnacle Strategies] came in, analyzed our problems, and within just a few days, gave us a recommendation and started the process on the very next [subsea] tree [product] in our assembly line. We cut almost 50% out of the cycle time of that tree assembly and we managed to hold onto that gain and continue to improve. That was impressive and we did it in just a matter of weeks."

FMC Energy Systems in Houston, Texas, maker of Energy Production and Processing Systems, is one of the businesses of FMC Technologies, Inc. (www.fmctechnologies.com), a global leader in mission-critical technology solutions. FMC Energy Systems produces Subsea Systems, Measurement Systems, Fluid Control Equipment, Loading Systems, Floating Systems, Blending and Transfer Systems, Surface Products and Material Handling Systems. For more information, contact them at 281-591-4000.

For particulars on *Pinnacle Strategies* and how their Constraint Management, Lean Manufacturing and exclusive signature methods improve the bottom line, call 972-491-1333 or visit www.pinnacle-strategies.com on the internet. Pinnacle works with organizations to improve organizational performance. Their primary specialties are: supply chain strategy and optimization, production scheduling, manufacturing operations strategy and scheduling, business process reengineering, project management and Critical Chain.

###

Thayer Bennett is an independent writer who specializes in industrial topics.

OTHER BOOKS ABOUT CRITICAL CHAIN

Leach, **Critical Chain Project Management (Second Edition).** Artech House 2005 (ISBN:1580539033)

Newbold, **Project Management in the Fast Lane: Applying the Theory of Constraints.** CRC Press (ISBN: 1574441957)

Nokes, Major, Greenwood, Allen, and Goodman, **The Definitive Guide to Project Management; the fast-track to getting the job done on time and on budget.** Prentice Hall (ISBN:0273663976)

Made in the USA